Dialectic of trauma
EXPERIENCE AND LANGUAGE

Dialectic of trauma

EXPERIENCE AND LANGUAGE

Edited by

LEKSHMI R. NAIR

Foreword by

GAYATRI DEVI

AUTHORSPRESS

Worldwide Circulation through Authorspress Global Network
First Published in 2022
by
Authorspress
Q-2A Hauz Khas Enclave, New Delhi-110 016 (India)
Phone: (0) 9818049852
E-mail: authorspressgroup@gmail.com
Website: www.authorspressbooks.com

Dialectic of Trauma: Experience and Language
ISBN 978-93-5529-018-2

Printed in India at Kensington Press

There is no life without trauma. There is no history without trauma . . . . Trauma as a mode of being violently halts the flow of time, fractures the self, and punctures memory and language.

Gabriele M. Schwab (2010, 42)

Acknowledgements

I am happy to acknowledge my sincere gratitude to all my friends and colleagues in the academia for their insightful advice, critical interventions and ardent support. Appreciation is due to all the contributors of the book who shared my passion for the project. My deepest gratitude goes to Professor Gayatri Devi who wrote the Foreword to the book.

I wish to thank the publisher, Authorspress, for being a part of this maiden venture. I am indebted to Nazrulla Mambrol and literariness.org for the beautiful cover design. I am thankful to Aparna Radhakrishnan for her meticulous proof reading.

Last, but not the least, I thank my family for their patience and encouragement and for providing me with a holding environment when I needed it the most.

Lekshmi R. Nair

Foreword

The successful liberation of trauma studies in the 1990s from its psychiatric and psychoanalytic contexts of emergence in the early half of the twentieth century helped frame, clarify and link the discontinuities and dislocations in the memories of violence and loss between the survivor who suffered the traumatic event, and their larger, broader, social, historical, political and cultural contexts. This expansion in the scope of trauma studies is necessarily a representational challenge: what purpose do trauma narratives serve and for whom and how? How do survivors negotiate the need for language and expression with the need to transcend the violence they lived through? What form do thoughts, memories and experiences of violence and suffering assume on the body and mind of a trauma survivor? How do societies accommodate, repudiate and negotiate trauma? Is trauma-induced repression necessarily aporetic?

The essays collected in the *Dialectic of Trauma: Experience and Language* explore narratives of acute violence and trauma, repression and survival, and eventual inscription and expression of the wounding knowledge across multiple modalities from oral testimonies, survivor interviews, journalistic coverage, fictional texts, films, and graphic novels. Theoretically framed and imaginatively unpacked through trauma-informed readings, these essays connect the historical and cultural exigency of narratives touched by violence for the contemporary lived realities of those transitioning through zones and sites of conflict from diverse regions of the world, be they geographically determined or ideologically engendered. From child abuse to transgenerational trauma to genital mutilation, from the performance of memory in narratives of violence to the grammar of trauma cinema, from Franz Kafka's Penal Colony to Margaret Atwood's Gilead to Alice Walker's Olinka, from Bhopal to Lebanon to Sri Lanka, the essays in this collection emphatically call attention to understanding and approaching individual trauma as an index of ruptured relations in the wounded body politic.

While trauma studies is a flourishing academic discipline in its own right, the addition of such a new collection as the *Dialectic of*

Trauma serves to underscore our renewed understanding of the historical interpretation of suffering, victimhood and survivorship. As the introduction to this collection asserts, our historical moment may be described as one informed by the "historiography of the vanquished." The present collection is a valuable addition to this project of corrective historiography where winning is often revealed as nothing more than the capacity to inflict suffering on another human being. Accurate depictions of such truths told from those who underwent great suffering to emerge out from under it are necessary for any imaginative envisioning of a just present. In giving voice to the stories of those touched by violence, *Dialectic of Trauma* contributes to such an ethical world building.

Gayatri Devi
Professor of English
Savannah College of Art and Design
Savannah
February 10, 2022

Contents

Introduction: On Reading the Wound

Lekshmi R. Nair

> Stories are told to register a truth that cannot be found in the simple telling of facts.
>
> Sue Grand, *The Reproduction of Evil*, 2002, 41.

The ceremonious emergence of trauma studies in the mid-1990s, with its distinct ethical and humanist understanding of the responses to extreme events and its subsequent evolution as a contemporary discipline, encompassing history, memory and culture, challenges our perception of the familiar precincts of human thought and experience. The concept of trauma entails a fundamental dislocation of the boundaries. Our understanding of psychology, sociology, history, psychiatry and literature has been repeatedly relied upon to complement our perception of traumatic events and the attendant responses they evoke on the victims, witnesses and perpetrators. "Trauma has become a major signifier of the age" (Fassin and Rechtman xi), where experiences of genocide, slavery, rape, terrorist attacks, natural disasters and catastrophes are singularly categorised and talked about, employing the same clinical and metaphorical language of trauma, "one signifier for a plurality of ills signified" (Fassin and Rechtman xi). The register of trauma is constantly employed to mark our understanding of human responses to unpleasant occurrences, both on an individual and a collective level. Since this domain of critical enquiry shares its boundaries and concerns with various other disciplines, the boundaries, scope and content of the field remain fluid and contested (Stevens 2011).

The Greek connotation of the term 'trauma' denotes physical injury from an external cause. In the mid-90s the term was used extensively to describe emotional or psychological injury as opposed to bodily harm. The violent events of WWI led to the development of severe symptoms in soldiers and war veterans, conceptualised variously as combat stress, shell shock, traumatic neurosis, and later grouped under the title Post Traumatic Stress Disorder, a condition that called for psychiatric and biomedical mediation. From mid to the late 19th century psychiatric and biomedical considerations of trauma categorised it as a disease of the mind, framing it as a pathological condition that necessitated professional therapeutic intervention. Trauma was seen as an "individual response of non-ordinary men confronted with basic ethical choices which they were unable to take on" (Fassin and Rechtman 62). The traumatised individual thus became the coveted subject of various theoretical and interdisciplinary practices that converged and expanded around his distressed life. Therapeutic practices were largely aimed at restoring normalcy and healing the vulnerable, wounded and fragmented psyche.

Trauma defines lived experiences in the "age of trauma" (Miller and Taugaw 2002). The Holocaust has been regarded as the paramount instance of collective trauma in the early days of the discipline. However, experiences of migration and displacement have gained prominence as potential sites of trauma, indicating a paradigm shift in the larger framework of trauma studies, especially towards the latter half of the 20th century. Trauma studies witnessed an epistemological shift in the late twentieth and early twenty first centuries with a veritable transgression into the realms of history, politics, memory and culture, and a positioning well within the disciplinary confines of the humanities and social sciences. The disjointed, traumatised self, hitherto the object of psychiatric and biomedical intervention, evolved into a cultural object, garnering popular critical and literary attention. Trauma becomes "a product of history and politics, subject to reinterpretation, contestation, and intervention" (Casper and Wertheimer 3).

The dialectic of trauma grants a unique status to human suffering, placing it above all other conceivable forms of pain and agony. The extensive theorisation of trauma by Sigmund Freud in the 20th century provided a psychoanalytic foundation for the analysis of trauma, revising our perception of trauma as an essentially pathological condition. Freud suggests that trauma is not a single experience of unpleasant events, but rather, trauma is the successive transition from an unpleasant experience to its repression to its return. Such experiences assume a traumatic force in their temporal delay. Freud points out that dreams occurring in traumatic neurosis have the characteristic of "repeatedly bringing the patient back into the situation of his accident, a situation from which he wakes up in another fright" (SE 18:13). Caruth refers to this as "the literal return of the event against the will of the one it inhabits" (1995 5), suggesting an "inherent latency within the experience itself" (18), an "incubation period" which Freud regards as "a transparent allusion to the pathology of infectious disease" (1939, 84).

The psychoanalytic and historical analysis of trauma seems to suggest an imminent departure from the site of trauma, from the original moment of occurrence. The inherent belatedness of trauma manifests itself in the listening of another, in the narration of trauma. In his essay "Beyond the Pleasure Principle" (1920), Freud illustrates the workings of trauma and maintains that an unpleasurable memory or trauma unconsciously repeats itself within its victims. The traumatised subject has a "passive experience, over which he has no influence" (14) and the traumatic subject relives in his present those unpleasant moments every time they are repeated in memory. Fassin and Rechtman in *The Empire of Trauma* observe that trauma has become a universal human experience, a constant which lies "in the moral economy of contemporary societies" (276). The dislocation of boundaries makes trauma an all-inclusive phenomenon and as Caruth states, "it brings us to the limits of our understanding... listening through the radical disruption and gaps of traumatic experience" (1995 4). Trauma introduces a new means of perceiving events, urging us to reconsider our notion of individual experiences and the ways in which these experiences are communicated to the outside world. The elementary dislocation implied by traumatic experiences suggests the impossibility of its direct access, and the language of trauma essentially reflects this inaccessibility, termed as its "textual 'undecidability' or 'unreadability'" (Craps 2013).

Trauma theory emerged as a distinct mode of literary and cultural analysis in the latter part of the 20th century. From its early origins in psychoanalysis and experiences of listening to the testimony of Holocaust survivors, trauma theory evolved into a broader discipline exhibiting a comprehensive understanding of narratives of violence and vulnerability. The varied focus and sensibilities of trauma theorists and the emergent interest in the discipline ushered in by the works of Caruth, Felman, La Capra, Leys, and Laub, reflected upon the interpretation of literary texts in ways that expanded and enriched our perception of both literary texts and trauma theory.

The therapeutic, literary and pedagogical modes of engaging with trauma assumed a new significance with the critical interventions of Cathy Caruth who theorised trauma as an event "outside the range of usual human experience" (1995 3). Caruth argues that trauma is "the confrontation with an event that, in its unexpectedness or horror, cannot be placed with the schemes of prior knowledge... and thus continually returns, in this exactness at a later time" (1995 153) to reenact itself at a later stage in the life of its victims. Caruth juxtaposes Freudian psychoanalysis, as outlined in *Moses and Monotheism* and *Beyond the Pleasure Principle*, with de Manian deconstruction and proposes that trauma resists representation and hence reflects its inherent inaccessibility. The poststructuralist turn in trauma theory regarded trauma as "the inaccessible truth of remembering" (Kansteiner and Weilnbock 231). Theorists like Caruth, Felman and Laub believed that trauma could only be "adequately represented through the use of experimental, modernist textual strategies" because of their "fragmented, non-linear, anti-narrative forms" which demonstrate "similarities with the psychic experience of trauma" (Craps 4-5). Caruth alludes to Laura Brown's acknowledgement of the "radical potential of psychoanalysis" to "retell the lost truths of pain among us" (1995 9). It is not just the moment of the unpleasurable event that assumes traumatic proportions for its victims, but rather the progression out of it – the very act of leaving the site of trauma becomes problematic.

Remembering, narrating and surviving trauma constitutes a new challenge for its victims as they experience a repeated suffering of the event every time the site of trauma is revisited. Recollecting and articulating the atrocities once banished to the utmost recesses of consciousness are central to the process of healing. Victims of trauma tend to live in denial, unable to utter aloud the violations inflicted upon their body and mind. Denial and repression of painful memories and forceful dissociation of oneself from the site of trauma are common survivor responses. As the unpleasurable experience repeatedly resurfaces with a might of its own, the victims realise the futility of living in denial. Their salvation lies in retelling the truth about their traumatic experience. Judith Herman states that the conflict between the will to deny horrible events and the will to proclaim them aloud is the central dialectic of psychological trauma (1997). The act of narration is a reenactment of trauma for its victims, survivors and witnesses, as they attempt to reconnect the fragments and reconstruct the past to make meaning of their present, trying to come to terms with an 'unspeakable' past.

According to Felman, trauma generates implications between literature and psychoanalysis. In *The Juridicial Unconscious*, she identifies Hannah Arendt's 1963 report on the Eichmann trial held in 1961 titled 'Eichmann in Jerusalem' and the 1985 French film, 'Shoah' by Claude Lanzmann as the two works that have "forced us to rethink the Holocaust in modifying our *vocabularies of remembrance*" (2002 106-107). Felman argues that both these works, which appeared several decades after the atrocities of WWII and more than two decades apart each other, transformed forever the way in which this historical event is perceived in contemporary times. These works capture and represent the Holocaust in an entirely new light, displacing the collective frameworks of perception and transforming the vocabulary of collective memory of the greatest genocide in human history, adding a new idiom to the discourse on Holocaust (Felman 2002). In the context of the Eichmann trial, she observes that the witness testifies through his unconscious body. The body invades the testimony of the witness, dramatically and wordlessly carrying it beyond the "cognitive and discursive limits of the witness' speech" (Felman 163). The body is thus placed firmly within the ambit of trauma studies.

Postmodern interdisciplinary research has unearthed the link between trauma and memory and its impact on generating notions of individual and ethnic identities. The place of memory in potential trauma narratives, as manifested in the recollections of survivors, witnesses and also perpetrators of trauma, in resolving various forms of trauma has been the focus of research, especially in the area of literature. As LaCapra points out, "the memory lapses of trauma and conjoined with the tendency compulsively to repeat, relive, be possessed by, or act out traumatic scenes of the past... in this sense, what is denied or repressed in a lapse of memory does not disappear; it returns in a transformed, at times disfigured and disguised manner" (1998 10).

With its roots firmly embedded in forms of individual as well as collective identity, trauma influences and determines the course of personal and collective identity formation. In *Trends in Literary Trauma Theory*, Michelle Balaev claims that contemporary literary trauma theory asserts that trauma creates a speechless fright that divides or destroys identity (149). Balaev talks about the nature of the transmission of transgenerational trauma and argues that personal trauma transmutes into 'transhistorical trauma' as these stories are transmitted from one generation to the next, defining "contemporary individual identity, as well as radical or cultural identity" (149). Transhistorical trauma establishes a parallel connection between the individual and the group indicating that the individual partakes in the trauma experienced by the historical group with which he shares his race, religion, gender or nationality, even after the lapse of several decades.

> Collective trauma is passed down to individuals in multifarious and refracted ways. Some lives are hit with catastrophic trauma over and over again; then trauma, with its concomitant strategies of survival, becomes a chronic condition. Defenses and denial become second nature; traumatic repetition becomes second nature (Schwab, 2010, 42).

The unpleasurable experience suffered by a historical group is experienced by a single individual as these events are enacted in the individual and collective memory. Balaev asserts that this process of transmission of trauma also works in reverse. Individual trauma can be passed on to a larger group with which he shares social, cultural or biological similarities (149). Marianne Hirsch uses the term 'post memory' to describe the relationship that subsequent generations have with the experience of their ancestors who were the victims, witnesses or survivors of individual, collective or cultural trauma. Later generations 'remember' these experiences of trauma by means of stories, images and behaviours among which they grew up (Hirsch 107). These experiences lie latent in the individual psyche and constitute memories in their own right. These inherited memories dominate the individual consciousness as he is exposed, at a very early stage itself, to the narratives of pain and suffering of his forebearers. The individual runs the risk of having his own stories and experiences displaced as past events continue to exert their influence on the present. "To grow up with such overwhelming inherited memories, to be dominated by narratives that preceded one's birth or one's consciousness, is to risk having one's own stories and experiences displaced, even evacuated, by those of a previous generation" (107). Hirsch asserts that the individual will subsequently be shaped by the traumatic events that elude narrative reconstruction and exceed comprehension.

Caruth emphasises the repetitive, timeless and unspeakable nature of traumatic memory (1996 4). She asserts that, trauma is not manifested in the simple violent or original event in an individual's past, but rather in the way in which its largely unassimilated nature returns to haunt the survivor in the future (1996 4). The victims of trauma constantly revisit the site of trauma, relive the crisis, and remain trapped in the past. In the case of unmastered trauma, the victim is repeatedly haunted by the original event as it were an eternal present (LaCapra 149). Ruth Leys takes an exception to Caruth's deconstructionist approach to trauma criticising Caruth's notion of the 'literality' of trauma and its close proximity to Paul de Man's notion of materiality. Leys maintains that the works of Bessel van der Kolk and Cathy Caruth betray a "fascination with, almost a relishing of, the currently modish idea that the domain of trauma is the unspeakable and unrepresentable" (2000 304). Stef Craps takes issue with the founding texts of the field for its failure to live up to "the promise of cross-cultural ethical engagement" (2) and can be regarded as paradigmatic of the post-colonial critique of Caruth's work. Kali Tal also accuses Caruth of being partial to the views of Euro-American thinkers and scholars, and thereby reinscribing Western colonialism on the body of the alien Other (1995).

As trauma translates into narrative, the vulnerable, violated self merges into biography. The body and the self are mutually implicated in that biography of vulnerability (Olesen 1992, 210). The body is a conspicuous presence in the imaginings of critical trauma studies. Clinical or psychological enquiries of trauma categorise it as a disruptive bodily or emotional experience. Elaine Scarry's *The Body in Pain* is a persuasive account of how traces of textuality construct and position bodies. Analysing torture and its implications for the lived, experienced body, Scarry draws out an ethics of the body in pain. Kaplan (2005) explores how trauma impacts the lives of individuals and entire cultures and nations. The primitive human urge to draw meaning from personal experience and communicate it to others applies itself in the narration of traumatic events resulting in artistic and literary modes of expressing the individual and collective experience. Thus the broader political and cultural contexts of trauma have a large influence on how trauma is represented in popular media and other cultural and artistic forms. Kaplan claims that every trauma has variant manifestations depending on the people involved, as individual responses to unpleasant events and an individual's experience of trauma are determined largely by socio-cultural positioning, personal psychic history and his/her direct or indirect presence at the site of trauma. Ruth Leys describes the genealogy of the concept of psychic trauma from the late 19th century to the present in her monumental work *Trauma: A Genealogy, From Guilt to Shame: Auschwitz and After.* In *History in Transit*, LaCapra places emphasis on the social and political significance of trauma studies.

Casper and Wertheimer note that critical trauma studies address "a set of centripetal tensions: between the everyday and the extreme, between individual identity and collective experience, between history and the present, between experience and representation, between facts and memory, and between the 'clinical' and the 'cultural'" (4). Critical trauma studies attend to the ways in which trauma "reveals and unsettles social and cultural classification systems" (6). The intersectionality of trauma with other disciplines places it firmly within the domain of 20th century humanities and social sciences. "Trauma offers an 'imminent' God, as it were, in which the humanities live and breathe through the practices and needs of people at the edges – of space, time, and subjectivity – moving forth and back through various borderlands" (6). This is exactly why trauma theory represents a new critical idiom that reads the silences and the voices grounded in experiences of pain, damage and violence that "demands a new mode of reading and of listening" (Caruth 1996 9). Speaking about the interdependency of literary studies and trauma theory, Roger Kurtz observes that the perspective, the lens and the language that trauma theory offers are potent tools for the analysis and interpretation of literary texts and their relative socio-cultural and political contexts. He argues that the insights offered by literary studies would be useful for understanding the dynamics of trauma (17). In fact, 'trauma' has value for literature as it offers "exegesis in the service of insights about human functioning"

(Hartman 544). Trauma theory has provided literature with a set of concepts that allow it to revisit traditional approaches to and assumptions about literary texts and also to connect with social issues at large. Trauma is, as Whitehead claims, "inherently linked to the literary in ways that it has not always recognised" (4).

Geoffrey Hartman's seminal essay 'On Traumatic Knowledge and Literary Studies' introduces trauma theory as a field "focusing on the relationship of words and trauma, and helping us to 'read the wound' with the aid of literature" (537). Hartman points to the ways in which trauma studies ushers in a new ethical as well as clinical awareness, facilitating a study of literature driven by "more *listening,* more *hearing* of *words within words* and a greater openness to testimony" (541), making the "literary object" more connected with the workings of a "blatantly political world" (543). The repetition of traumatic memory and the subsequent transgenerational transmission of trauma culminate in the creation of a distinct identity, for the individual and for the group. "The recognition of trauma is crucial because it gives name and shape to a form of experience that is a rupturing of the capacity to make sense of the world" (Atkinson 5). Studying trauma in literary or cultural terms is to concern oneself with the "tension between what is known and what is not known" and also to be concerned with the "impact and dynamics of the woundedness and machinations of trauma... in all its reverberations.... This is what brings the study of trauma to the uncertainty of truth, the impossibility of bearing absolute witness to catastrophe, the multiplicity of historical narratives" (Atkinson 5). Every reconstructed narrative is a recreation of history, narrated from the exclusive vantage point of a witness, a survivor, a victim, or a perpetrator of trauma.

Mapping the Collection

This book, titled *Dialectic of Trauma: Experience and Language,* attempts to trace the dialectic of trauma and its multifarious manifestations. The experience of trauma often translates itself into a language of unfathomable depth and precision. The book looks at the various aspects of traumatic experiences, their narration and its implications for humanity at large. Priya K. Nair in "Trauma as Social Performance" mulls over the concept of social trauma and discusses the clinical, psychological and political aspects that are at work in the creation of the discourse. Nair argues that imagination informs the construction of the experience of trauma. Placing in context the works of Svetlana Alexevich she explores the pivotal role played by memory in the narration and construction of social trauma. As memory and trauma translate into the cyber space with the intrusion of technology in the process of dissemination of memory narratives, the notion of trauma as social performance assumes a new significance.

In the chapter "The Scared and the Scarred: Childhood Abuse and Trauma in Life-writing and Postmodern Visual Culture", Arunlal K. details how cultural sites have configured and narrated childhood trauma with special reference to representations of childhood in comics, life narratives and contemporary cinema. Building on Suzette Henke's concept of scriptotherapy and the narrative exteriorisation of trauma, the author argues that the expression of trauma requires the subject to use language. Analysing the extra-linguistic ways in which trauma imprints upon an individual's consciousness, the author establishes that trauma manifests itself better in visual codes. Rajesh V. Nair ruminates on the political and social aspects of trauma in "Muted Voices and Fractured Memories: Debating Trauma in Select Narratives from South Asia". The author interrogates the concerns of cultural trauma studies such as narrative voice, agency and its denial, de-centered subjectivities and double victimisation as represented in Echara Varier's *Memories of a Father* and T. D. Ramakrishnan's *Sugandhi Enna Andal Devanayaki.* The counter-hegemonic nature of these narratives culminates in a reframing of memory and the construction of sub-nationalist spaces.

The unconscious trail that trauma leaves, inflicting pain and a sense of victimisation in the survivors and their successive generations is categorised as transgenerational trauma. The 'unspeakability' of trauma translates itself into the lived experiences of future generations, informing their perception of their individual as well as collective history. Joji John Panicker analyses the nature of the transmission of transgenerational trauma in the chapter "Transmission of Trauma in Dystopian Fiction: A Study of Margaret Atwood's *The Handmaid's Tale* and *The Testaments*". The legacy of trauma is transmitted as silence, survival techniques and resistance across generations. The fragmented, non-linear, incoherent, and destabilising narrative structures of modernist and postmodernist literary texts best capture the innate literariness of the traumatic experience. Panicker concludes that transgenerational trauma can be a very persuasive and effectual agency of confrontation, rebellion and emancipation in a totalitarian and oppressive world order. The chapter "Trans-generational Transmission of Collective Trauma and Memory: A Reading of Leila Abdelrazaq's *Baddawi*" by Kochurani Joseph attempts to explicate the traumatic nature of refugee childhood experiences. The coming-of-age graphic narrative, *Baddawi*, poignantly captures the collective suffering of the historically traumatised Palestinian community. The collective memory and trauma passed on to successive generations define the group's cultural and historical identity. Joseph states that the Palestinians cling to the collective memory of a traumatised past as a cherished possession which facilitates the construction of meaning around an experience of extreme adversity. She argues that the transmission of trauma serves to restore the trans-generational collective self, as they negotiate the construction of an individual as well as shared historical identity.

The chapter "Aesthetics and Experience: Spatio-Temporal (Dis)locations in Postcolonial Trauma Cinema in India" investigates the ways in which trauma cinema captures and represents the fluidity of traumatic experience, the spatio-temporal dislocation of trauma and the rupture it entails. The author, Smitha M, states that the fluidity of the cinematic medium is congenial to the representation of the unthinkable, undecipherable nature of trauma. The trauma-ridden narratives enhanced with visual embellishments and cinematic techniques like flashbacks, mise-en-scene, mise-en-shot and montage, and positioned firmly within specific socio-historical and political contexts, augment and restructure our perception of historical and cultural trauma. Smriti M. Venugopal embarks on an in-depth analysis of the implications of witnessing trauma inscribed on the bodies of victims in "Witnessing Trauma Inscribed upon Bodies: The Dichotomy of Experiences in Franz Kafka's *In the Penal Colony*". The body attains centrality as trauma evolves into a spectacle. The corporeal self is the object, the site where trauma is painfully engraved. The body comes alive in torture, communicating a consciousness and an acute awareness of a disjointed subjectivity. The witness, caught in a web of vagueness and perplexity, identifies both with the victim and the perpetrator of traumatic violence.

Trauma narratives take their readers on a similar course, rendering a violent, dehumanising spectacle that confronts their capacity to witness and endure trauma.

Navya Chandran investigates Suroopa Mukherjee's attempts to comprehend the cultural memory of Bhopal gas victims in "History, Memory and Testimony: Gendered Victimhood and Post Traumatic Vulnerability in Suroopa Mukherjee's *Surviving Bhopal*". Oral testimonies, newspaper reports, pictures and monuments reconstruct the cultural memory of a collective trauma. Historical accounts of the event that exist as oral testimonies by women are used as an interface to establish the connection between official versions of the tragedy and lived experiences of trauma and suffering. Chandran concludes that these oral narratives explicitly point towards experiences of gendered victimhood and reconstruct a more humane and inclusive version of an unpleasant lived social reality. "'The Unkindest Cut': Female Genital Mutilation in Alice Walker's *Possessing the Secret of Joy*" is a take on one of the most pertinent markers of cultural significations practiced on the female body. The intense physical agony and the psychic trauma that the practice inflicts on women are culturally sanctioned in some African communities. Its force as a social construct and the forced commonality of the custom make women subject themselves to the trauma of violating their body and mind. The authors Indu V. Nandakumar and Geethu V. Nandakumar observe that the fragmented nature of the narrative mirrors the ruptured psyche, dislocated from the self, the society and the world at large.

Reinhardt Koselleck, the German historian observes that short term history is made by the victors; however, in the long run it is the history of the vanquished that becomes the accepted version (2002). Humanity's engagement with time and history has changed profoundly in the contemporary era. And "our view of the future, once full of hope grounded in the invocation of a new world order, has turned to disenchantment" (Didier and Rechtman 275). The legacy of trauma on our minds and bodies is so devastatingly lethal that it is impossible to regard historical events with complacency. We look back on history with wounded minds and bleeding eyes. Our relationship with the past has turned traumatic and tragic. From being the story of the victors, history has become, as Koselleck predicted, a "historiography of the vanquished" (Koselleck 2002;

Didier and Rechtman 275). Writing trauma has offered us a new critical idiom to talk about the wounds of the past and make sense of the present. Trauma has redefined our notions of time and history, repoliticising its victims and reinforcing the moral legitimacy of their suffering.

Works Cited

Atkinson, Meera, et al., *Traumatic Affect.* Cambridge Scholars Publishing, 2013.

Balaev, Michelle. "Trends in Literary Trauma Theory". *Mosaic: Journal for the Interdisciplinary Study of Literature,* vol. 41, no.2, 2008, pp. 18-149.

Caruth, Cathy. *Trauma: Explorations in Memory.* John Hopkins UP, 1995.

.... *Unclaimed Experience: Trauma, Narrative, and History.* John Hopkins UP, 1996.

Casper, Monica J., and Eric Wertheimer. editors. *Critical Trauma Studies: Understanding Violence, Conflict, and Memory in Everyday Life.* NY UP, 2016.

Craps, Stef. *Postcolonial Witnessing: Trauma Out of Bounds,* Palgrave Macmillan, 2013.

Fassin, Didier and Richard Rechtman. *The Empire of Trauma: An Inquiry into the Condition of Victimhood,* translated by Rachel Gomme. Princeton UP, 2009.

Felman, Shoshana. *The Juridical Unconscious – Trials & Traumas in the Twentieth Century: Trials and Traumas in the Twentieth Century.* Harvard UP, 2002.

Freud, Sigmund. *The Standard Edition of The Complete Psychological Works of Sigmund Freud.* Vintage, vol. 18, 2001.

.... *Moses and Monotheism,* translated by Katerine Jones. Knopf, 1939.

.... Beyond the Pleasure Principle, 1920.

Hartman, Geoffrey H. "On Traumatic Knowledge and Literary Studies." *New Literary History,* vol. 26, 1995, pp. 537-63.

Herman, Judith. *Trauma and Recovery: The Aftermath of Violence – From Domestic Abuse to Political Terror.* Basic Books, 1997.

Hirsch, Marianne. "The Generation of Postmemory". *Poetics Today,* vol. 29, no. 1, 2008, pp. 103-128.

Kansteiner, Wulf and Harald Weilnböck. "Against the Concept of Cultural Trauma (or How I Learned to Love the Suffering of Others without the Help of Psychotherapy)". *Cultural Memory Studies: An International and Interdisciplinary Handbook,* edited by Astrid Erll, et al., De Gruyter, 2008. pp. 229-240.

Kaplan, E. A. *Trauma Culture: The Politics of Terror and Loss in Media and Literature.* Rutgers UP. 2005.

Koselleck, R. *The Practice of Conceptual History: Timing, History, Spacing, Concepts,* translated by T. S. Presner et al., Stanford UP, 2002.

Kurtz, J. Roger. *Trauma and Literature.* Cambridge UP, 2018.

LaCapra, Dominick. *History in Transit: Experience, Identity, Critical Theory.* Cornell UP, 2004.

.... *History and Memory after Auschwitz,* Cornell U P, 1998.

Leys, Ruth. *Trauma: A Genealogy*. U of Chicago P, 2000.

Miller, Nancy K., and Jason Tougaw. "Introduction: Extremities." In *Extremities: Trauma, Testimony, and Community*, edited by Nancy K. Miller and Jason Tougaw, U of Illinois P, 2002, pp. 1-24.

Olesen, Virginia. "Extraordinary Events and Mundane Ailments: The Contextual Dialectics of the Embodied Self." In *Investigating Subjectivity: Research on Lived Experience*, edited by Carolyn Ellis and Michael G. Flaherty, Sage, 1992, pp. 205-20. Sage.

Schwab, Gabriele. *Haunting Legacies: Violent Histories and Transgenerational Trauma,* 2010, p. 42

Scarry, Elaine. *The Body in Pain: The Making and Unmaking of the World.* OUP, 1987.

Stevens, Maurice. "Trauma's Essential Bodies." In *Corpus: An Interdisciplinary Reader on Bodies and Knowledge*, edited by Monica J. Casper and Paisley Currah, Palgrave Macmillan, 2011. pp. 171-86.

Tal, Kali. *Worlds of Hurt: Reading the Literatures of Trauma.* Cambridge UP, 1995.

Whitehead, Anne. *Trauma Fiction.* Edinburgh UP, 2004.

CHAPTER 1

Trauma as a Social Performance

Priya K. Nair

In Greek language the word Trauma means, "wound", which is physical in nature, but in contemporary usage the word signifies mental and emotional wounds as well. Traumatic experiences can be entirely personal or it may affect an entire community. Experiencing natural calamities, wars or accidents, which involve a community can be called 'social trauma.' In such situations trauma may be both personal and private, yetat the same time, it is an experience that is collective. Traumatic experiences are narrated after an interval of time and such narrations are termed testimonies. The world outside comes to know of such experiences mostly through these mediated narratives. The testimonies depend on the memory of the person who is narrating, but there are many factors that have impact on memory.

When trauma is discussed, one needs to break away from the disciplinary silos that constrain one's understanding of the event. Social trauma is both clinical and political and the psychological aftermath and the politics involved in creating the discourse should be looked into carefully. To comprehend the various dimensions of social trauma and the testimonial narratives that are based on the event that caused the trauma it is necessary to look at the space in which the event occurred and the socio-political context in which it happened and the political structures that engaged with the event. The psychological aspects of the traumatic experience naturally demand medical knowledge and the cultural understanding of mental health in the specific geo local context to understand the event and the interior experience of the event. The political structure that was in place at the time of the event is also crucial. This is important not just because it reveals the cause of the event and how it was dealt with but also as it has a role to play in the discourses that are generated based on the event. The memory of the event, the testimonies that are narrated and the discourse that is created and disseminated – all these factors are found to be heavily influenced by the existing structures of power and the ideology that this power structure depends on. Trauma as a phenomenon creates an interdisciplinary space for itself. It starts a movement to illustrate the phenomenon of change caused by an injury; suffering and pain are narrated or performed and this often helps the victim to reach a point of self-knowledge and achieve an altered worldview. It can be ameliorating or it can result in a thirst for revenge.

Personal suffering can be intense and is cause for intellectual as well as moral concern and therapy. It is mostly of interest to psychologists or to writers of fiction, but collective trauma draws a wide variety of players into its network. Individual responses to traumatic injuries may be varied. It can be repressed and denied or it might be narrated to get relief. The victims may be able to actualise the pain and mourn. Mourning is a therapeutic process, which brings relief to troubled minds. Disastrous experiences experienced by entire communities may not always be understood, projected or internalised as collective trauma. It is evident that social or collective trauma though real has to be symbolically projected, constructed and disseminated. The sense of connection must be forged among the victims and also connect with the target audience. In order to achieve this connection narratives and images are used. The notions of 'Us' or 'We' are coded into the social fabric. This collective identity experiences danger, assumes the victim status and identifies the perpetrator: This results in a joining of forces against a perceived danger or threat.

History is filled with events of collective suffering caused by many types of disasters. We see that the past was marked by several wars, famines, floods, epidemics and genocides – all of which were traumatic to the people who went through these experiences. Some of them were natural disasters and certain others were caused by humans. The impact of imperialism and exploitation, slavery, racism, gender based and caste-based violence, intense religious factionalism was brutal. Such events are categorised as 'collective trauma' as there occurs a paradigm shift in the world view of the individuals who have experienced it. Collective traumatic experiences are often attributed to the wounding of a particular social identity that is claimed by a group or a community. "Cultural trauma occurs when members of a collectivity feel they have been subjected to a horrendous event that leaves indelible marks upon their group consciousness, marking their memories forever and changing their future identity in fundamental and irrevocable ways" (Alexander1).

Traumas, we then understand, become collective, only if they are conceived and projected as wounds inflicted upon the identity of a particular group of people. The identity again is a construct that has been naturalised by cultural practices. Suffering groups must be homogenised and their victimhood must be represented and projected into the minds of the target audience, thus we can see that social or cultural trauma is a discourse that is constructed and sustained through multiple modes of dissemination.

It has been seen time and again that all massive disruptions in a society are not experienced as trauma. It is imperative to understand how an event becomes a traumatic one and is categorised as collective trauma at that. Representations of the specific event have a crucial role to play in creating an experience that can be seen as trauma. The understanding that one has been traumatised by an event is constructed in different ways by different people. Each person might have undergone the same experience in a slightly different manner. As trauma is a psychological experience, the inner life of a person is impacted along with physical wounding. The concept of social trauma also carries within itself a move for amelioration. The paradigm shift that occurs in the world view may result either in a demand for revenge or it might lead to efforts seeking solace.

Cathy Caruth, in *Unclaimed Experience*, problematises trauma by referring to its psychological impact. She writes that it is not the experience itself that produces traumatic effect, but the remembrance of it, so there is an interval of time during which the victim may forget. But it is by a reflective process by which memory links the event and the experience of trauma. So, the trauma is reenacted through memory and performed as testimony. As the reflective process is set in motion the human mind links the event that happened in the past to the present through representations that use imagination to a certain extent. The memory of the past is filtered through imagination and ideology.

Trauma seems to be much more than a pathology, or the simple illness of a wounded psyche: it is always the story of a wound that cries out, that addresses us in the attempt to tell us of a reality or truth that is not otherwise available. This truth, in its delayed appearance and its belated address, cannot be linked only to what is known, but also to what remains unknown in our very actions and our language (Caruth17).

Narratives based on trauma rely on the memory of the event. But memory is fluid and fallible as numerous memory studies have proved. Like trauma studies, the study of memory is a convergence field where a number of disciplines like cultural history, social psychology, media archaeology and political philosophy contribute their systems of knowledge. Literature too has a major role to play in the study of memory. Cultural memory according to scholars is of a social nature which relates past and present and the future taking into consideration socio cultural and political structures. Cultural memory is both a process of remembering as well as forgetting. It has individual and collective dimensions and these cannot be separated.

The sustaining and dissemination of memory is crucial to cultural memory of a trauma that is seen as collective. Max Weber termed as "carrier groups" (Weber 468–517) the set of agents who are engaged in the process of recreating the traumatic incident. These groups claim to represent the group and collect fragmented experiences and generate discourses to validate claims of social trauma. In the days before globalisation and the easy availability of technology the carrier group and the target audience were caught within the same social web and would have had the same experiences of the event. But as time passes the demography of the target audience as well as that of the carrier group would change. The discourses generated after the event carry the seeds of memory that may project it as a collectively experienced traumatic event that had created an undeniable impact on the collective consciousness of a people. Hence the study of trauma must consider the narratives of trauma that are available in multiple forms. Such narratives are politically motivated and project the victims and the perpetrators in a simplistic binary. Social trauma is powerful enough to bring together heterogeneous groups and generate a feeling of oneness among them. This can also cause a sense of moral responsibility to grow within a community. But studies of social trauma have found that not all collective experiences were experienced or projected as social trauma and often this silencing is also deeply political.

Several definitional accomplishments must be made before an event can qualify as a cultural trauma. It must be remembered, or made to be remembered. Furthermore, the memory must be made culturally relevant, that is, represented as obliterating, damaging, or rendering problematic something sacred – usually a value or outlook felt to be essential for the integrity of the affected society. Finally, the memory must be associated with a strong negative affect, usually disgust, shame, or guilt (Smelser 36).

It therefore becomes clear that the social or cultural trauma is performed and sustained through multiple modalities of discourses. Usually in the beginning stages of the process of creating the discourse of trauma most people who have not experienced the event do not feel any connection with the victimised group. Vicarious trauma is the project of stories and images. So, the representation of the victims is crucial, as they have to be shown to share certain valued qualities so that the larger audience outside the trauma network can symbolically and vicariously experience the social trauma. Another point to be underscored is that the group needs to remember that their social identity was harmed. Jeffrey C. Alexander lists the criteria that define the nature of the trauma that has been experienced; they are the nature of the pain, nature of the victim, relation of the victim to the wider audience and attribution of responsibility (13-15).

History and literature have projected the Holocaust and the Nazi regime as massive instruments of genocide, but we also have to understand that imperialism and slavery had also unleashed extreme modes of exploitation on non-western people by the hegemonic western powers. In western countries the Holocaust is highlighted and the world vicariously shares the pain inflicted on the Jews. So, it is imperative to inquire why the trauma experienced by certain groups is ignored or repressed. An example of how social trauma has been obscured is narrated by Iris Chang, "Even by the standards of history's most destructive war, the Rape of Nanking represents one of the worst instances of mass extermination" (Chang 1997, 5). The Battle of Nanking was fought in December 1937 during the Second Sino-Japanese War between the Chinese National Revolutionary Army and the Imperial Japanese Army for control of Nanking, the capital of China. It was terribly traumatic for the people who lived in Nanking, but according to Chang it became "the forgotten Holocaust of World War II," and it remains an "obscure incident" today (6).

For political or social reasons carrier groups have not successfully been able to disseminate this traumatic experience and to generate a discourse regarding this event. So, their experience is obscured from public view and has not found a place in public memory and for this reason the moral responsibility for causing this suffering has not been accepted by the perpetrators neither has solidarity been extended to the victims from a wider group of people. There are other reasons too as to why all traumatic experiences are not imagined as collective traumas.

At times the event instead of wounding social identity actually strengthens their homogenous identity. "Americans who sent soldiers to triumphal victory in the World Wars I and II did not experience collective trauma, despite the tens of thousands of deaths to men and women they loved and lost. Neither did Germans during their early Blitzkriegs. The reason was that these lost lives, far from endangering American and German collective identities, actually reinforced them (Giesen 2004). This can be seen in the instance of freedom struggles that were launched in erstwhile colonies. The struggles of the freedom movement in India brought a heterogeneous community together under the complex idea of the nation state. The traumatic experiences heightened the resistance and created heroes.

Another reason for the erasure of cultural trauma is the conflict within the society itself. In the postwar period individuals recorded their sufferings in many ways. There were intensely personal diary entries, letters, photographs and coded narratives. Giesen has documented that in cities like Hamburg which were heavily bombed, ceremonies were held to commemorate the disastrous event. But as Alexander and Breese write in the Introduction to *Narrating Trauma: On the Impact of Collective Suffering*, "these representations of the bombings never amounted to an authoritative representation orienting collective political and moral perceptions" (xiv). They further elaborate that the trauma projected by post war Germany during the occupation was compared to the horrifying atrocities of the Holocaust, and the 'war-guilt narrative' became stronger and more vivid in the eyes of the audience. The individual sufferings of thousands of Germans did not become the nation's collective narration. The nation that had suffered war crimes could not in this instance take up the victim status." Many Germans commemorated their soldiers' suffering at the Battle of Stalin-grad well into the 1960s; it was only the rise to preeminence of Holocaust memory that made such trauma construction of German military sacrifice impossible" (Alexander XV).

Anti-Semitism had always existed in the west but the carefully documented Holocaust actually resulted in institutionalising Jewish suffering and it appeared that their trauma was shared even by people who had not been part of this torture. This injury has been sustained over generations and across most countries. But we see that the Holocaust was reconfigured in many Arab countries. The creation of Israel set in motion another wave of anti-Jewish feeling. Palestinians and many Islamists all over the world strongly challenged the reality of the Holocaust. So, there is clearly another performance that denied the event totally. But the Jews in Israel and outside continued to keep the memory of the trauma alive. They used multiple modalities of rituals, narratives and used the cyber space to its fullest extent to ensure the continuation of memory. They succeeded in reviving ancient experiences of exploitation. Literary texts were read revealing the discourse of anti-Semitism in them.

A traumatic event, as it has been seen, can generate emotion to an extent where national boundaries are blurred but at the same time it can also serve in strengthening the feeling of nationalism. It is in this context that one can read Arthur Neal's definition of "national trauma" in *National Trauma and Collective Memory: Major Events in the American Century* as a response to events "which cannot be easily dismissed, which will be played over again and again in individual consciousness" and which then become "ingrained in collective memory." This is seen in Anderson's notion of *Imagined Communities* (1983) as well. If Anderson used the idea of fiction as a binding force it can be seen that the discourse of national histories is created around events that have injured the social, moral and cultural fabric of ethnic groups. There is an awakening towards perceived injustice and a cry for revenge. When the nation state is in crisis or when the idea of homogeneity is questioned, perceived trauma provides a platform for collective identification, the Indian freedom movement being a case in point.

It is often found that nationalists, core right wing groups and the media that they control assume the victim position asserting that they were traumatised by certain other rival groups and calling for strong modes of resistance. Many such movements can be discerned in the contemporary globalised world. Historical events are referred to, events that have been recorded and documented, but these events are interpreted from a particular perspective. A group's interests are foregrounded. Though History and the framing of events in historical narratives are supposed to be more objective than individual or collective memory we find that the historian's ethnicity and political predilections often colour the narrative regarding the event.

A close reading of the initial reports on what was later called the Holocaust shows that it was not projected at that time as such a horrendous violation of human rights. Jeffrey C Alexander notes that, "In the beginning, in April 1945, the Holocaust was not the "Holocaust."" (197). He writes that the first reports that appeared in America during the Second World War had not, referred to the actions by German Nazis, or the Jewish victims, but to the Japanese army's brutal treatment of American and other allied prisoners of war. It was much later that the reports of genocide started emerging. It is in this context that we must raise the question of symbolic production of trauma: Who controls the means of symbolic production? In the case of Nazi atrocities, for a long period of time as the world war raged, the Nazis themselves were in full control of the geographical terrain, the modes of cultural production and the media. But if one looks at the actions of the Allies it can be seen that the images of torture in concentration camps started emerging.

The contingency of this knowledge is so powerful that it might well be said that, if the Allies had not won the war, the "Holocaust" would never have been discovered. Moreover, if it had been the Soviets and not the Allies who "liberated" most of the camps, and not just those in the Eastern sector, what was discovered in those camps might never have been portrayed in a remotely similar way. It was, in other words, precisely and only because the means of symbolic production were not controlled by a victorious postwar Nazi regime, or even by a triumphant communist one, that the mass killings could be called the Holocaust and coded as evil (Alexander 203).

Discourses which emerged succeeded in establishing the Nazis as the embodiment of all evil and Hitler gained notoriety as one of the worst dictators the world had ever seen. But one should remember that most European powers at the same time were unleashing extreme forms of torture on their colonies. But these images were not available in the public domain and hence the vicarious trauma was not experienced at that point of time and even when such narratives started emerging, they did not achieve the global reach and identification that the images of Jewish suffering had captured.

Atrocities that were unleashed upon the natives in the Belgian Congo were brutal. A book written by Adam Hochschild titled *King Leopold's Ghost: A Story of Greed, Terror, and Heroism in Colonial Africa* is a factual account of Leopold's cruel ways. The book raises the question whether the king was the first ruler in modern times to embark on a mission of genocide and it also points out that he may have been responsible for the death of more Africans than the number of Jews who were killed by Nazis. The point that this example makes clear is that social and cultural trauma needs to be performed before it gains acceptance. Vicarious trauma just like that experienced by the audience of a tragic play is dependent on the construction of the trauma narrative. Hochschild claims that ten million people may have died in a 'forgotten holocaust.' Hochschild's narrative has been repeatedly challenged claiming that the atrocities he described were largely exaggerated but they fail to account for the fact that the population of the Congo shrank after Leopold took over, though exact figures are hard to establish.

Studies on the September 11 attack on the twin towers in the U.S clearly show us the nature of the social and cultural trauma of a nation that was projected and sustained through the imaginations of the carrier groups. The twin towers that symbolised American capitalism and military domination of the world were destroyed by the Al Qaeda. The nation as one accepted the trauma and the victimhood of America. Comparisons were made to the Japanese attack on Pearl Harbor, which had occurred exactly sixty years earlier. The nation as a single entity went into mourning. The people of America felt that the country for them would never be the same again; this also strengthened America's war against terror. This act of terrorism it seemed legitimised America's involvement in the affairs of any country that they considered were indulging in terrorist activities. Great efforts were made to sustain the memory and certain words came to represent the attack on America. 9/11 had many connotations but it was appropriated to refer to the twin tower attack alone. 9/11 became a code in fact to refer to the attack. Ground Zero only meant the point directly above, below, or at which a nuclear explosion occurs or the center of rapid, violent activity but now the term 'Ground Zero' is taken exclusively to refer to the twin towers. The people who visit ground zero in Manhattan like pilgrims hope to see the spot where the attack occurred and there are relics available in the form of the letters of support, hats and T-shirts. These symbols ensure sustained memory of the event.

A country which is the hub of capitalism and has global power finds it relatively easy to project its internal trauma as the trauma of the world and there too making a clear differentiation between countries that propagate terrorism and those that fight against terrorism. In a subtle manner it put forward a binary that the good countries were all with America and they took it upon themselves to label the other countries as those which encouraged terrorist activities. In this context it is crucial to examine what is known as vicarious trauma. In the intensely globalised and technologically enhanced world the media projects visuals and that too, at times, live image of catastrophes all over the world. This leads to a situation where people experience trauma vicariously through the media images rather than directly. This is what was set in process with the proliferation of the images of the twin tower attack.

For the first time perhaps on such a large scale digital media platform played an essential role in disseminating trauma. The accessibility and global reach they have turned them into important means of processing trauma through the establishment of online communities. As Kaplan wrote "the digital media turned out to be a major information outlet through which the global audience was connected to the destruction of the World Trade Center" (12).

The visuals of the catastrophe were transmitted via TV and the Internet to a global audience. The collapse of the twin towers resembled the scenes of a Hollywood movie. The visuals gained an iconic status much like the mushroom cloud of World War II. Those who interpreted 9/11 in terms of its traumatic impact stressed the gap between the immediacy of the media images and the ability of the public to make sense of the events, or even to believe what they were seeing. However, the sense that the events had somehow already been visualised before they happened suggested the appropriateness of an approach that drew from Freud, who had emphasised the role of fantasy and desire in the construction of events as traumatic (Meek 13). If in the post Holocaust period the Nazi regime and Hitler emerged as forces of evil the Al Qaeda and Osama Bin Laden unleashed a culture of fear even among people who had only seen the attack on their TV screens. The bout of islamophobia that emerged was then only to be expected.

Cultural or social trauma is paradoxical because even when the event is real, imagination informs the construction of the experience of trauma. There may be two types of memory at work here. One is the personal memory, which is recreated, in the form of a testimonial narrative and the other involves the process of representation of the trauma using imagination even when one has not directly experienced the event. Claims to victimhood may not be validated even if it is perfectly justifiable. So, when one goes deep into the idea of social trauma, we need to be aware of the agents who create a discourse that validates and morally justifies the victimhood of the traumatised people. These agents or carrier groups may be intellectuals, politicians, journalists or writers and the claims about the nature of the wound, the victim and the perpetrator may be different. The victim, the exploiter and the audience are drawn into what has been called powerful 'accusatory narratives, 'but the narratives may be conflicting especially in the case of the accusations that are made and a careful reading can show us how one specific narrative carrying a particular political ideology gets the attention of the audience. This decision to give a particular perspective predominance depends not just on the narrator but also on the demographics to the target audience. Barry Schwartz writes, "given the constraints of a recorded history, the past cannot be literally constructed; it can only be selectively exploited" (398).

Books on history can tell us there were stories that were valorised and validated and those that were repressed and later forgotten. Carrier groups have to narrate and ritualise the event. They do it in multiple ways; create monuments, write poems and stories and perform plays to re-enact the traumatic event. By using all these devices, they ensure that they keep the wound fresh in the minds of the target audience. Even a very superficial knowledge of the mass-media makes us aware that there is a filtering of facts and this leads to selective construction of events. So, the event is caught within a web of interests and what emerges is often a highly politicised, coloured version of the incident. The perpetrator, victim and the nature of the incident are constructed through the prism of ideology and the disseminated narratives influence the public. So, it is evident that the discourse that emanates involves several strategies. The testimonial narratives are used to heal the public psyche but also to keep the memory alive. It also serves to interpret the past so as to lay the foundation for an expected future.

Film theorist E. Ann Kaplan proposes that "trauma produces new subjects" (Kaplan 1); that is, it produces new forms of political identification based in different experiences of victimhood, shared suffering and witnessing. "Despite the proliferation of images of war, torture, genocide and natural disaster in Western news media, certain events, such as the Holocaust or 9/11, have become iconic cultural traumas – relived and retold in numerous documentaries and dramatisations. Commentators suggest we are living in a "trauma culture" in which "extremity and survival are privileged markers of identity" (Luckhurst 2).

As testimonial narratives depend on the memory of the event one should understand the concept of memory and the dynamics of processing that goes on in the mind of a person who has experienced the event. "Memory has three meanings: the mental capacity to retrieve stored information and to perform learned mental operations, such as long division; the semantic, imagistic, or sensory content of recollections; and the location where these recollections are stored" (Young 5).

Memory is the ability to conceive of the past as the present. Individual memory and collective memory may be at odd with each other at times. A social trauma that is performed as collective memory may need to transcend the individual memory and creative a shared experience in the minds of the people. … "collective memory provides the individual with a cognitive map within which to orient present behavior. In this sense, collective memory is a social necessity; neither an individual nor a society can do without it" (Eyerman 66).

Memory is collected and represented through language and through symbols. Testimonial narratives play with the counters of memory and imagination. Memory narratives are also known as forensic mode of writing about the past. This type of writing focuses on events that may not be located in the distant past and hence must take into account the memories of the victims of the trauma. Memory Studies, examines the representations of the past and why we remember it that way. As memory has a fundamental role to play in the narration of trauma research into individual and social memory is mandatory. The field of Memory Studies foregrounds the relationship between memory and the future as well.

As Elie Weisel writes "If the Greeks invented Tragedy, the Romans the Epistle and the Renaissance the Sonnet, our generation invented a new literature that of testimony" (3). Literature and film can vividly portray memory whether it is personal or collective. The genres of literature aestheticise testimonies using techniques like symbolic systems, metaphors and at times such modes even defamiliarise the event. Literature has a number of memory narratives that have been powerful texts about wars, genocides, slavery and colonialism. The experiences of the two world wars were enshrined in multiple modes of narratives; fiction, poetry, theatre and film. Camus' *The Plague* and Dostoevsky's *Notes from the Underground* are narratives that have explicated their positions during the events that caused trauma. Camus' doctor-witness-narrator feels compelled to narrate the tragic events that he saw unfold. Dostoevsky speaks about the time he had served as a prisoner in Siberia. As Adorno himself said "I have no wish to soften the saying that to write lyric poetry after Auschwitz is barbaric …. It is still in art alone that it can still find its own voice, consolation without being betrayed by it" (312).

The number of poems about the world war bears testimony to this statement. Narratives can be explicitly testimonial or it can symbolise trauma in an abstract manner. Anne frank's Diary can be considered to be an explicit testimonial about the Nazi atrocities. On the other hand, in *Waiting for Godot* (1954) Samuel Beckett portrayed the absurd and psychologically traumatised life of the modern individual created after the Second World War. It also portrays the brutal impact of capitalism. Beckett represents the types of individuals who have lost their perception of time and the meaning of their existence. In India a number of novels captured the trauma of partition. The narratives often explicitly discussed the experience of partition but at times the projection was symbolic. As Professor Vinay Lalin one of his talks commented, the Hindi movies in the seventies mostly dealt with the theme of families being ripped apart, and finally reuniting in the climax. This was a projection of the angst caused by partition and the solace they found was the coming together of the family when they were certain that the two countries would never come together (Talk at St. Teresa's College, August 2018).

It is in this context that a writer like Svetlana Alexevich becomes crucial to the problematic of memory, narration and the construction of a social trauma. She reveals the extraordinarily fragmented nature of memory. Her texts reveal the fluid nature of human memory.

Alexievich's books make up a series that she calls "The Chronicle of the Big Utopia, or The History of the Red Man." Each book deals with an event that wreaked havoc on a large number of people. Her literary method blurs the genres of history and imagination. Oral narratives are collected from witness-participants or their surviving family members and she puts together these testimonies that reveal the contradictory manner in which human beings recollect a specific event that happened in the past. She interviewed 500 to 700 people asking them to recollect the same event and their lived experiences.

Chernobyl Prayer is a series of oral narratives that attempt to document the nuclear disaster. We can compare it to a series of witnesses narrating their experiences. The writer relegates her own voice to the margins of this book. We hear the author's voice very rarely. Alexievich begins with a brief history of the event and there is an epilogue. In a chapter called "The author interviews herself on missing history and why Chernobyl calls our view of the world into question" (33). Svetlana Alexievich makes it clear that this is not a book about the details of what happened at Chernobyl, why the reactor failed, who was to blame, etc. Instead, she writes: "What I'm concerned with is what I would call the 'missing history', the invisible imprint of our story on earth and in time. I paint and collect mundane feelings, thoughts and words. I am trying to capture the life of the soul" (33).

The book contains multiple monologues of people who lived near Chernobyl, worked on the cleanup, saw loved ones die from radiation, etc. They are a heterogeneous group of people, there are atomic scientists, doctors, politicians and engineers, and ordinary people who experienced the 1986 meltdown of the Chernobyl nuclear plant in northern Ukraine and the subsequent radiation. What is striking about the text are the official versions that spun a different narrative. The writer speaks to former communist leaders who were in charge then and their word tell us how the power structure controls and filters information and for this reason the text is storehouse of memories that would otherwise have been erased from public memory. Alexievich, through her narratives, serves to establish the fragility of memory and the projection of discourses regarding events that are conceived of as traumatic.

In the contemporary technologically adept world, the concept of trauma has to be looked at from the perspective of digital memory as well.

> The visual media do not just mirror those experiences; in their courting and staging of violence they are themselves the breeding ground of trauma, as well as the matrix of understanding and experiencing of a world out of joint. The visual media have become a cultural institution in which the traumatic experience of modernity can be recognised, negotiated, and reconfigured (Kaplan and Wang 17).

Meek has written extensively on the "traumatic image," (40)a stark image of someone or something that is brutally attacked, murdered or tortured. This iconic image stands for the event as such. A picture as we all know has the power of a thousand words and such traumatic images can shock even a viewer who has not experienced the specific trauma. Sontag writes about the production and consumption of information via modes of technology: "In an era of information overload, the photograph provides a quick way of apprehending something and a compact form of memorising it" (Meek 22). But this has another dimension as well. Media proliferation results in the numbing of senses and the viewer insulates against the negative impact of such images.

The Covid-19 pandemic has many of the characteristics that define the notion of cultural trauma, a disruption of mundane routine of daily life that was taken for granted, distrust of strangers, lack of faith in the abilities of the power structure, intensive negative reporting in the media, conflicting ideas that try to give meaning to the disaster and an incredulity towards the achievements of scientific knowledge. The difference that Covid-19 pandemic marks from the other traumatic incidents in history is that humanity all across the world have experienced this devastation though in varying degrees and with varied modalities of victimhood. It is a bio political condition and has shaped both individual and collective identities at the same time. This is important, as the geo local context of the victim is crucial in deciding the extent of her or his experience.

The discourses about the pandemic are replete with accusatory narratives, it shows world leaders drawing military lines around their nations and the idea of democracy is challenged as the power structure legitimises itself by withholding basic citizen rights. The culture of fear has become stronger than before, if it was fear of the other in pre Covid times, the pandemic has ushered in the fear of the virus as well. The Covid-19 trauma has been represented in new forms of artistic expression and as if signaling future times, the chosen modes are mostly virtual.

The cultural memory in the present is formed and sustained in the cyber space and like Alexevich's experimental narratives the cyber space is inundated with conflicting and at times, contradictory narratives. So, unlike in the past, the repression of the memory of a particular class or group is not going to be an easy process. It is likely that memory studies and the idea of social trauma as a performance will be in an altogether different mode when technology is factored into the process of remembering and the dissemination of memory narratives. Technology it has been seen has impacted human memory in an unprecedented manner. Technology has brought about huge changes in our everyday life, the way we read has changed so has the mode of writing, and research has suggested that it may have profound effects on our memories. It would be difficult now to think of a social performance of trauma that does not involve technology. The notions of memory, testimony and performance would need to be revised keeping in mind the possibilities of technology and its reach.

Works Cited

Adorno, Theodore. *The Essential Frankfurt School Reader.* Continuum, 1982.

Alexander, Jeffery. "Toward a Theory of Cultural Trauma." *Cultural Trauma and Collective Identity*, edited by Jeffery Alexander et.al., U. of California P. 2004. pp. 1-31.

Alexevich, Svetlana. *The Chernobyl Prayer.* Penguin Books, 2005.

Anderson, Benedict. *Imagined Communities.* Verso, 1991.

Beckett, Samuel. *Waiting for Godot: A Tragicomedy in Two Acts.* Grove Press, 1954.

Breese, ElizabethButler, et al. *Narrating Trauma: On the Impact of Collective Suffering.* Taylor & Francis, 2015.

Camus, Albert. *The Plague.* Vintage International, 1991.

Caruth, Cathy. *Unclaimed Experience.* John Hopkins UP, 1995.

..........*Trauma Explorations in Memory.* John Hopkins UP, 1995.

Chang, Iris. *The Rape of Nanking: The Forgotten Holocaust of World War II.* Penguin, 1997.

Dostoevsky, Fyodor. *Notes from the Underground.* Eartnow, 2017.

Eyerman, Ron. *Cultural Trauma: Slavery and the Formation of African American Identity.* Cambridge UP, 2001.

Giesen, Bernhard. *Triumph and Trauma.* Paradigm Publishers, 2004.

Hochschild, Adam. *King Leopold's Ghost: A Story of Greed, Terror, and Heroism in Colonial Africa.* Macmillan, 2019

Kaplan, E. Ann. *Trauma Culture: The Politics of Terror and Loss in Media and Literature,* Rutgers U P, 2005.

.... and Wang, Ban, editors. *Trauma and Cinema: Cross-Cultural Explorations.* Hong Kong U. P,2004.

Luckhurst, Roger. *The Trauma Question.* Routledge, 2008.

Meek, Allen. *Trauma and Media.* Routledge, 2010

Neal, Arthur G. *National Trauma and Collective Memory: Major Events in the American Century.* M. E. Sharpe, 1998.

Schwartz, Barry. "Deconstructing and Reconstructing the Past." *Qualitative Sociology* 18(2). 1995, pp. 263-170.

Smelser, Neil J. "Epilogue: September 11, 2001, as Cultural Trauma." *Cultural Trauma and Collective Identity*, edited by Jeffery Alexander et. al., U. of California P, 2004, pp. 264-283.

Weber, Max. *The Protestant Ethic and the Spirit of Capitalism.* Translated by Talcott Parsons, Charles Scribner's Sons, 1958.

Weisel, Elie. *Dimensions of the Holocaust.* Northern U P, 1977.

Young, James E. *Writing and Rewriting the Holocaust: Narrative and the Consequences of Interpretation.* UP, 1990.

CHAPTER 2

The Scared and the Scarred: Childhood Abuse and Trauma in Life-writing and Postmodern Visual Culture

Arunlal K.

Childhood – a temporary state – becomes an emblem for our anxieties about the passing of time, the destruction of historical formations, or conversely, a vehicle for our hopes for the future. The innocent child is caught somewhere over the rainbow – between nostalgia and utopian optimism, between the past and the future (Chris Jenks, *Childhood*).

Of late, narratives on childhood and childhood-trauma have been getting published to high critical and popular acclaim. This trend has been on a high internationally since the 1990s. Authors like Mary Karr, Frank McCourt, and James McBride surfaced in the mid-1990s, and set this trend of narrating the child. These authors focused on narrating the child with reference to the trauma they had to survive – these narratives focus on abuse, impoverishment, neglect, and identity crises. In the last twenty years the world has witnessed more than five hundred autobiographies by children or young adults. The idea of child has developed much over these decades: a rising number of documentaries and films about children, childhood and childhood trauma, in effect, brought to children a social agency that history had never conceded to them before.

Narratives of this nature have also appeared on social media profusely. Blogs, Facebook and twitter have become spaces for adolescents to share their traumatic experiences. The fact that the children themselves are doing it there has an element of empowering, in that they somehow command better control on how their lives are to be represented.

The present paper connects trauma studies and representation of childhood in life narratives, comics and contemporary commercial cinema to explore the ways in which cultural sites have configured childhood and narrated it. This paper considers life narratives as cultural allegories to develop a better understanding of the various ways in which childhood is constructed. Susanna Egan writes in generally about the confusion between autobiography as a genre and memoir and life narrative:

We are politically and theoretically short-sighted when we quarrel with a term as comprehensive and as flexible as "autobiography." I recognise that each alternative term has been introduced either as a form of resistance to the exclusionary practices of traditional humanism, and part of a valuable reshaping of the field, or in what I think of as a mistaken understanding that this or that curious item that has caught our attention does not really belong. With the field of autobiography studies radically reshaped over the past twenty years, my concern now is that we reach for new horizons not as separate or contested territories but as significant features of the landscape, protecting ourselves from anxiety about what does or does not belong by acknowledging the flexibility of a word that admits so many variations (Mirror Talk 14). The paper therefore uses the term "autobiography" interchangeably with "memoir," "life writing," and "life narrative." In the context of the study, these terms are anyway, semantically closely related.

A discussion on the autobiographising of childhood should perhaps start from how an adult author conceptualise events from his or her childhood. Narratives of childhood is a practical subgenre of autobiography, occupied by writers of literary and popular autobiography, by academics, celebrities, therapists, and social activists. Their representation of traumatic childhoods is a conspicuous trope in their studies – particularly autobiographical depictions of child abuse. The linkage between life-narrative and children's trauma has made the genre famous and notorious at once. There is no doubt that, autobiographies of childhood have brought child abuse to public attention and have researched on tools of resistance; on the other hand, these books were taken to task for their eroticism, voyeurism, violent idiom and so on.

It must be noted that the narratives of childhood trauma as a major readerly genre came of age as the world took a turn to the precious child era. Internationally, there happened a resurgence and reappraisal of the child-figure. The United Nations Convention on the Rights of the Child demanded in the beginning of nineteen nineties for "a deeper cultural awareness of children's rights." Children are not the rightful property of parents or guardians. This move has brought about much change in the way childhood was perceived in cultural outputs internationally.

In India, specifically, since the 1990s and 2000s childhood has been highly visible at all levels of popular cultural life from art and literature though advertising, popular television programs, and films. Further, as Henry Jenkins argues, the child figure has been, and continues to be, important in a range of political and ideological battles; in fact, he contends, "almost every major political battle of the twentieth century has been fought on the backs of children" (2). Jenkins's assertion is well supported by a cursory glance at political events of the 1990s and 2000s. A number of "flash points" relating to Western childhoods have marked the late twentieth century and the early twenty-first as a time when childhood was "in crisis." Henry A. Giroux used "flash points" to refer to "moments of social crisis, which can be seen to challenge or consolidate specific aspects of cultural memory that surround childhood" (269). In the "stranger danger" era, people were being asked to consider the plethora of diverse and complex relationships that exist within families.

As a consequence, most of the movies and life narratives that focus on children have placed their focus on family. Usually, child abuse occurs when the family or agents of the family such as babysitters, family friends, or trusted family connections such as clergy transgress the space of children (consider the autobiographies of Andrea Ashworth, Constance Briscoe, Augusten Burroughs, Duncan Fairhurst, Antwone Fisher, Donna Ford, Rosalie Fraser, Mary Karr, and Dave Pelzer, to name just a few examples).

That children are capable of violence is an idea that clearly falls outside traditional formulations of childhood. Children were traditionally marked as are either innocent or evil and, "innocent" children were said to be under pervasive threat from "evil" children. Incorporating the insight that violence need not be figured as an experience of outside the agency of childhood kicked off a turn to traumatic autobiographies of childhood. These narratives indicate a new global culture preoccupied with trauma and guilty childhoods. These narratives, whether films or literature, are deeply imbued with the preoccupations of the present – children's rights, children's futures, education, violence against and by children, socialisation, and childhood sexuality, to name just a few pertinent examples. Individual lives become emblematic of wider social concerns about childhood. One could consider autobiographies of childhood as a tool of cultural memory. Cultural memory is the innumerable ways in which so-called individual memory is socially and culturally shaped – for example, by institutions, cultural myths, and traditions. Cultural memory also encompasses challenges to official or historical memory – for instance, facilitating the emergence of new or counter-memory. Consider the ways in which autobiographies of childhood function to both "corrupt" and "protect" childhood (to appropriate Jenkins's terms).

Autobiographies of childhood have had tangible social impact: they have formed part of a network of cultural texts that have impacted upon social justice for children. For instance, autobiographer Kathleen O'Malley has written on the abuse she underwent in an Irish industrial school managed by the Sisters of Mercy in the 1950s, in her autobiography *Childhood Interrupted.* O'Malley now works with survivors and has publicly campaigned for an apology from the National Society for the Prevention of Cruelty to Children (NSPCC), the Irish government, and the religious organisations that failed to protect her as a child. Representation of childhood through life-writing is a contemporary vogue. But the practice has a significant past and a traceable genre-evolution.

As a genre, life-writing of childhood goes way back in history. And a reading of the same in contemporary times need to be informed by this past – particularly, the reading of the genre as a means of "writing back" to paradigmatic historical representations of childhood. Of particular significance has been the gradual shift that the genre has made from primarily contesting childhood being a space for the exploration of an artist's development to being a space for exploring and celebrating the independent cultural function of childhood and for highlighting the experiences of the traumatised child.

The modern autobiographers tried to understand childhood as a social evolution and explored how experiences of childhood influence adult life. For example, in *Hunger of Memory: The Education of Richard Rodriguez*, Rodriguez analyses the sidelining he felt as a Mexican immigrant kid in the United States. This in essence becomes his key experience to shape his adulthood. In Bollywood movies such as *Highway* directed by Imtiaz Ali and *Monsoon Wedding* by Mira Nair, the same theoretical precise used to extend the trauma of the childhood extending to intervene in the protagonists' adult life and decision making. Mira Nair's approach is comparable to many film narratives and life narratives of childhood produced in the recent years. The narrators and the film makers commonly use the life of children as a launch pad for exploring social history.

The mid-1990s saw the publication of three notable autobiographies of childhood: Mary Karr's *The Liars' Club*, Frank McCourt's *Angela's Ashes*, and James McBride's *The Color of Water*. Generally, these texts have been cited as serving the reason for the boom that followed. What is distinctive about this grouping is that each of the texts represents a lower-socio-economic experience of childhood, and each depicts trauma. Each represents a rags-to-riches journey from a poor childhood and unconventional family life to adult success. Karr's *Liars' Club* represents the effects of adult dysfunction – alcoholism, violence, mental illness, neglect, and rape – on the children that witness this dysfunction and inevitably 10 contesting childhood become implicated within it. Karr's autobiography was widely praised for its wit and lack of self-pity. McBride's *Color of Water* was also praised for its lack of self-pity, but most notably this autobiography was commended for its exploration of racial identities and its celebration of McBride's resilient mother. *Angela's Ashes* – McCourt's autobiography of his poor, miserable Irish childhood – became one of the literary success stories of the 1990s. McCourt's autobiography is presented as an accessible, "real-life," rags-to-riches narrative reconstruction of childhood from a child's perspective, addressing issues such as poverty, alcoholism, domestic violence, and infant mortality.

Autobiographies and life writings have of late received much cultural and critical attention. The term 'first person era' has been credited to twenty first century by cultural observers thanks to this development. As mentioned earlier, this period has also been a boom period for writing about childhood. Media also brings to us a range of 'other' children besides wistful depictions of child-like beauty and innocence, such as "street kids," child prostitutes, drug and substance addicts, and rebels pertaining to politics and more. *Udta Punjab*, and

Kahaani 2 are two recent films that represent these troubled children in their narratives. In these films, we find diverse children: both victims and perpetrators of violence; refugees and victims of disasters. Stolen children, abused ones and murdered children are also part of many of these narratives. Most of these films are inspired by true events. In some cases, at least they have used news stories that attracted nation-wide attention for their plots. The number of such films are on a high and they have gone on to make a special category of visual life-narratives.

More specifically in postmodern visual culture, artists like Phoebe Gloecknerhave explored the possibility of narrating childhood traumas. Gloeckner uses the medium of graphic novels and comics to communicate the childhood sexual trauma. Gloeckner happens also to be one of the most controversial narrators of the same. Gloeckner's books, *A Child's Life* and *The Diary of a Teenage Girl* have often been cited as superb postmodern cultural instances to understand how life-writing can use more diverse platforms such as comics and not mere prose narratives to narrativise trauma. Gloeckner's representation of childhood abuse trauma had made critics to generally focus on the feminist edges of the whole process: how it excites and simultaneously shocks the reader and his fantasies. It has also been understood as a variant narrative of resistance to patriarchy. However, the fact that such works as these offer a revolutionary metamorphosis to the representation of trauma in life-writing still calls for critical attention. The formal properties of comics autobiography that she resorts to offer unique opportunities for the representation of the scenes that she remembers from her period of trauma.

Gloeckner has been a medical illustrator most of her life though she had been trained to draw ever since childhood. *The Diary of a Teenage Girl* (2009) is an attempt to give visual manifestation to a journal she had kept during her teenage. On cross-checking one could see that half of what she has given in the comic book is exactly what is written in the diary years back. Butit should come as a surprise that Gloeckner has repeatedly refused to identify the comics as an autobiography or even a fictionalised autobiography. She wants the *The Diary* to be primarily read as a work of creative engagement with the source material. In this respect Gloeckner has been a far cry from artists such as Alison Bechdel, Marjane Satrapi and Art Spiegelman, and the ilk who has insisted on the autobiographical fidelity of their comics/graphic novels. Gloeckner begins The Diary saying "this account is entirely fictional and if you think you recognise any of the characters as an actual person, living or dead, you are mistaken" (iv). She denies formally that something as pictured had actually happened. Not just that: she has also gone on record as to how she never used authentic snippets from her diaries to draw her comics. She has repeatedly denied that she draws for life into the comics. In this, her position coincides with that of contemporary theoreticians on life-writing.

However, Gloeckner has also warned us about the authenticity of the materials. It is true that she had used her diaries. But she has also brought much padding narratives to the traumatic anecdotes: "sometimes you have to distort 'reality' in order to express what you feel is the true feeling. A recounting of facts can carry little meaning. An artist imposes a certain order on perception" (Groth 179).

Leigh Gilmore, a contemporary writer whose interest falls in life-writing studies proposes that "the autobiographical project may swerve from the form of autobiography even as it embraces the project of self-representation"(3). Unlike earlier ideas regarding life-writings, the newer theorists doubt whether the genre is as naturally affiliated to history or factuality as it was thought to be. They say the reader shall "submit to a fiction" when "offered some kind of cohesion of the writing 'subject' which is guaranteed by the writing signature, by the name which is attached to the text"(Smith 104). As Smith and Watson has observed, This double fiction, which "(...) first presents an autobiographical narrative that is inescapably shaped by a subject that in turn is considered fragmented, incoherent and a product of discursive identity-formation, means that critics have often considered it more helpful to approach autobiographical telling as a performative act" (Smith & Watson). The performance of the self in autobiography can thereby in important ways be constitutive of subjectivity, as the writer creates a unified representation of a largely fictional self from the available discursive resources. In this light, one could understand autobiography, as an "opportunity for self-transformation" (Gilmore, 11). It is an experiment in creating another inside one's own self.

It is imperative therefore to understand the specific contexts that various aspects of visual culture offer autobiographers. Unlike cinema or documentary, the comic narrative takes a linear movement (or a deliberate breaking of it) through drawn up panels separated by gutters. It has traditionally not taken up life-narrations. But the evolution and contemporaneity of the form, and furthermore, the emergence of forms like graphic novels have changed the scene. In this connection we should also remember scholars like Jared Gardner who put the truth-function of life-writings:

> The comics form necessarily and inevitably calls attention through its formal properties to its limitations as juridical evidence – to the compressions and gaps of its narrative (represented graphically by the gutter space between the panels) and to the iconic distillations of its art. The kinds of truth claim that are fought over in the courts of law and public opinion with text-based autobiography are never exactly at issue in graphic autobiography. The losses and glosses of memory and subjectivity are foregrounded in graphic memoir in a way they never can be in traditional autobiography (Gardner 6).

Comics is not a genre very conducive to create autobiographies in the traditional way. Its distribution of narrative and spirit works differently. Comics by default constructs a world that allows the flaring up of fancies and fantasy unlike the prose counterparts where the writing person is expected to extend the real and the historical in a narrative. Prose autobiographies are in this respect, less a means to float trauma than a means to host truth-function. To depict traumatic autobiographic segments, one might as well think of comics or other non-prose means. Especially in the case of people whose subjectivity has not been favorably appraised by the society, unconventional means of life-narrations open up a plethora of diegetic possibilities. It is therefore not accidental that life-writings such as the ones made by Gloeckner resorted to non-prose narrative modes. The narrative expectations from a comic narrative get exploited to graft painful and traumatic life-instances. In fact the future of life-writing will be dependent more on how non-prose representations can carry childhood or subaltern or feminist traumas through to the readers.

Ruth Leys observes that PTSD (post-traumatic stress disorder) is recognised by the American Psychiatric Association as a condition of mental fragmentation and schizoid subject:

> The idea is that [...] the mind is split or dissociated: it is unable to register the wound to the psyche because the ordinary mechanisms of awareness and cognition are destroyed. As a result, the victim is unable to recollect and integrate the hurtful experience in normal consciousness; instead she is haunted or possessed by intrusive traumatic memories (Leys 2).

The autobiography of the traumatised subject is therefore going to be in different degrees distanced from a straightforward narration of what happened to him or her. The fragmented way in which things gathered in the subject's memory needs to be put together to make a coherent narrative. Usually, the subjects of trauma who narrate their autobiography therefore rescript the whole experience. There will be new narrative lines and plot-bifurcations that can pad up and accommodate the fragments that the trauma had produced and scattered.

The necessity to project out trauma is a major pre-requirement in most treatment procedures. Judith Lewis Herman would even go to the extent of stating that: "In the telling, the trauma story becomes a testimony" (181). Shoshana Felman, quoted by Suzette A. Henke, also supports this stance when she argues that "a surrogate transferential process can take place through the scene of writing that allows its author to envisage a sympathetic audience and to imagine a public validation of his or her life testimony" (Henke xii). In the same manner, Dori Laub emphasises the role of the witness in the process of working through traumatic memories", may it be at "the level of being a witness to oneself within the experience [or at] the level of being a witness to the testimonies of others" (Laub 61). That traumatic people need to speak out is a theory that has trickled down from the days of Freud and scholars such as Herman have argued that scriptotherapy – the narrative exteriorisation of trauma – is a major part of the treatment of trauma even today. Extending Herman's ideas Henke proposes that "the object of psychoanalysis – and of autobiography as scriptotherapy – is to 'reassemble an organised, detailed, verbal account, oriented in time and historical context' out of 'fragmented components of frozen imagery and sensation.'" (158) Getting the traumatic pieces of the experiences out of a person requires the subject's using language. But it is also significant that the primary impact and the evolution of the traumatic experience were not exclusively linguistic in nature. It has plenty to do with extra-verbal stimuli and semiotics.

Scholars such as Bessel A. van der Kolk and Onno van der Hart have tried to crack the extra-linguistic ways in which trauma stamps itself in a person's consciousness. In fact, as fragments, false memories, sublimated memories and nightmarish experiences, trauma manifests better in visual codes. Kolk and Hart say, "cognitive psychologists have identified three modes of information encoding in the CNS [central nervous system]: inactive, iconic and symbolic/linguistic" (172). Since trauma can be generally understood as "a frightening event outside of ordinary human experience," theoreticians say that the victims "experience a 'speechless terror'" which "cannot be organised on a linguistic level, and this failure to arrange the memory in words and symbols leaves it to be organised on a somatosensory or iconic level" (6-7).

Films such as *Udta Punjab*, *Kahani 2*, *I Am*, *Page 3*, *Highway*, *Monsoon Wedding* or *Gunday* that have tried to narrate lives of abused children (some of them inspired by news events) represent trauma in a more than mere verbal way, as it is done in traditional autobiographic narratives. Kaplan has noted that the abuse victims "put their experiences in writing [...] for several reasons: to organise pain into a narrative that gives it shape for the purposes of self-understanding (working their trauma through), or with the aim of being heard, that is, constructing a witness where there was none before" (20). With films the trauma becomes a witnessed event and not a mere narration. The participation of the audience as sympathizers synchronised with the film also is a factor to consider. Such films open us to the possibility that the hidden abuse does not just stop at being a scar in a person's memory, instead it debilitates their very faculty of using language to expose the abuse. Visualisation is a collective process. Making a film out of a narrated trauma adds a whole lot of other serious semiotic layers to the representation of trauma. The format of a film allows the narrative to develop a seamless drafting off scattered memories. In fact, it is more effective than the paneling in the comic books. The visual lay out of the traumatic narrative in that sense leads to a healing as well, both within for the person who attempts that and without for the ones who consume it.

Conclusion

The paper tried to put together various theoretical and field-work knowledge about representation of childhood trauma. Ever since 1990s literature and non-literary narratives have shown growing interest in children, childhood and the depiction of children's life. In fact, children's life-writing itself came of age as a veritable genre during this period. The paper searched the reason why such a surge in interest happened during the time. It found that there were policy regulations from the part of UN and that there were several social evolutions that foregrounded the child figure during that era. The narratives on children's traumas were also starting to use other semiotic systems such as comics and films. The paper explored the connections and points of departures among these various representational logics.

Works Cited

Amazon.com. "Customer Reviews" for James McBride, *The Color of Water: A Black Man's Tribute to His White Mother* 21 June 2008. www.amazon.com.

Ashworth, Andrea. Interview with BBC i. n.d. 8 Nov. 2002 www.bbc.co.uk/health/hh/inter02.shtml.

.... Interview with Douglas Eby. n.d.18 Nov. 2001 www.creativityandwomen.com/article1025.html

.... Interview with Louise Jameson. n.d. 8 Nov. 2002 www.open2.net/everwondered1/image/topic3.html

.... Interview. "Writing from Life: Exploring Contemporary Writing about Childhood."18 Nov. 2001 www.englishandmedia.co.uk.

Deman, J. Andrew. "The Intervening 'I': Phoebe Gloeckner's Comics Memoir and the Destruction of Visual Pleasure," *American Visual Memoirs After the 1970s: Studieson Gender, Sexuality, and Visibility in the Post-Civil Rights Age*, ed. Mihaela Precup. U of Bucharest P, 2010.

Egan, Susanna. "Changing Faces of Heroism: Some Questions Raised by Contemporary Autobiography." *Biography: An Interdisciplinary Quarterly,* vol. 10, no. 1,1987, pp. 20-38.

.... *Mirror Talk: Genres of Crisis in Contemporary Autobiography.* U of North Carolina P, 1999.

.... *Patterns of Experience in Autobiography.* U of North Carolina P, 1984.

Gardner, Jared. "Autography's Biography, 1972-2007," *Biography,* vol. 31, no.1, 2008.

Gilmore, Leigh. *The Limits of Autobiography: Trauma and Testimony.* Cornell UP, 2002.

Giroux, Henry A. "Stealing Innocence: The Politics of Child Beauty Pageants." *The Children's Culture Reader, edited by Henry Jenkins.* NYUP, 1998, pp. 265-282.

Gloeckner, Phoebe. *A Child's Life and Other Stories.* Frog, 2000

.... *The Diary of a Teenage Girl.* Frog, 2009.

Groth, Gary. "Interview: Phoebe Gloeckner," *The Comics Journal,* vol. 261, 2004.

Henke, Suzette A. *Shattered Subjects: Trauma and Testimony in Women's Life Writing.* St. Martin's P, 2000.

Herman, Judith Lewis. *Trauma and Recovery.* Basic Books, 1997.

Jenks, Chris. *Childhood.* Routledge, 1996.

Jenkins, Henry, editor. *The Children's Culture Reader.* NYUP, 1998.

Kaplan, E. Ann. *Trauma Culture: The Politics of Terror and Loss in Media and Literature.* Rutgers UP, 2005.

Karr, Mary. *Cherry*. Picador, 2000.

.... *The Liars' Club: A Memoir*. Picador, 1995.

Laub, Dori. "Truth and Testimony: The Process and the Struggle," *Trauma: Explorations in Memory*, edited by Cathy Caruth. Johns Hopkins UP, 1995.

Leys, Ruth. *Trauma: A Genealogy*. U of Chicago P, 2000.

McCourt, Frank. Angela's Ashes. HarperCollins, 1996.

O'Malley, Kathleen. *Childhood Interrupted: Growing Up under the Cruel Regime of the Sisters of Mercy*. Virago, 2005.

Parker, Alan, director. *Angela's Ashes*. Universal, 1999.

Rodriguez, Richard. *Hunger of Memory: The Education of Richard Rodriguez*. Bantam, 1983.

Rosenberg, Meisha. "Multimodality in Phoebe Gloeckner's Diary of a Teenage Girl," *International Journal of Comic Art*, vol. 9, no.2, 2007.

Smith, Paul. *Discerning the Subject*. U of Minnesota P, 1988.

Smith, Sidonie and Julia Watson. *Autobiography: A Guide for Interpreting Life Narratives*. U of Minnesota P, 2010.

van der Kolk, Bessel A. and Onno van der Hart, "The Intrusive Past: The Flexibility of Memory and the Engraving of Trauma," *Trauma: Explorations in Memory*, ed. Cathy Caruth. Johns Hopkins UP, 1995.

Washington, Denzel, director. *Antwone Fisher*. Fox Searchlight, 2002.

CHAPTER 3

Muted Voices and Fractured Memories: Debating Trauma in Select Narratives from South Asia

Rajesh V. Nair

In the narratives of trauma, we may see a preoccupation with its psychological dimensions. Therefore, taking a different trajectory, the paper debates the social and political aspects of trauma with a focus on South Asia. By proposing a broad theoretical framework of the 'cultural memory studies' approach to analysing trauma, I propose to highlight the diversity and heterogeneity in the South Asian context, touching on its myriad realms such as gender, and ethnicity. Aspects of cultural trauma studies, such as the notion of agency, which includes questions such as who narrates the traumatic experiences, victims or narrative subjects, denial of agency and de-centred subjectivities, and double victimisation, etc. will be addressed. Equally significant is the infiltration of trauma into popular imagination through narrative representation, verbal as well as visual. The production of sub-nationalist or 'counter-spaces' (Lefebvre 32) and the process of the political formation of subjectivity is also worth exploring. Here, aspects of sovereignty, human rights, and the performance of the body as a cultural signifier are important. Ultimately, what we witness through these texts is a reframing of memory and a rethinking of the nation.

As we know, the term 'trauma' has its roots in Greek, which means 'wound,' particularly an injury inflicted on the body, but later, with the development of psychoanalysis, Sigmund Freud extended it to "a wound upon the mind" (Caruth3). In fact, she defines trauma as an "enactment of a belated experience" (7) which has an "endless impact on a life" (CUE 7). Caruth elaborates further:

> In its general definition, trauma is described as the response to an unexpected or overwhelming violent event or events that are not fully grasped as they occur but return later in repeated flashbacks, nightmares, and other repetitive phenomena. Traumatic experience, beyond the psychological dimension of suffering it, involves, suggests a certain paradox: that the most direct seeing of a violent event may occur as an absolute inability to know it; that immediacy, paradoxically, may take the form of belatedness (91-92).

Trauma theorists such as Luckhurst, Mandel, Yaeger, and Visser have addressed the social and political implications of trauma in their ways. However, traumatic experiences can be narrated in different modes but each one has its peculiarities. In *Trauma: Explorations in Memory*, Caruth continues,

> There is no single approach to listening to the many different traumatic experiences and histories we encounter, and that the irreducible specificity of traumatic stories requires in its turn the varied responses – responses of knowing and of acting – of literature, film, psychiatry, neurobiology, sociology, and political and social activism (ix).

Memory is a symbolic or metaphoric representation of the unbearable, and it may not be taken as an accurate description of an event[1]. Traumatic memory is the result of the inner workings of the mind; the fantasy which is created through that act is full of elisions, interruptions, and reinventions. Here, one may distinguish between traumatic memory and narrative memory for a better understanding of trauma. As Caruth argues, traumatic memory takes so long time to communicate, unlike narrative or ordinary memory, because it is a "solitary activity" (163) not addressed to anyone. Secondly, there is no social component in traumatic memory, unlike narrative memory, which is essentially a "social act" (163), a mode of communicating the unspeakable experience to readers. Besides, narrative memory is subjective as it is structured by individual mental constructs with ideological underpinnings.

Traumatic narratives of memory contest the past, and they help as corrective forms of history and even problematise nation-making. For instance, T. V. Eachara Varier's memoir *Memories of a Father* (2004) exposes the brutal oppression of the state during the emergency period, muffling all sorts of dissent; in fact, the missing body of his son Rajan[2] during the notorious emergency period for his alleged involvement in the Naxalite movement[3] is a dark episode in Kerala history. The memoir reframes public memory by bringing in an alternate reading of the incident which challenges the official, state version. The memorial turns out to be a counter-text, a counter-memorial narrative when he claims:"...the fathers of our judicial system were that particular that no innocent person should be punished wrongly. But today our enquiry officers never care a damn whether the real culprits or the innocent are the ones punished" (23).

Memorials are often erected as an act of remembering; statues of important figures such as Gandhi or Patel generate discourses around them. Paul Connerton in *How Societies Remember* (1989) drives home the myriad narratives such as "commemorative ceremonies and bodily practices" (7) which help in configuring social memory. However, the formation of social memory leads to collective identity formation. Cultural memory, as Jan Assmann puts it, is formed with the help of several narratives, (verbal as well as visual) which act as' cultural texts' in inscribing collective memory. In fact, they are 'memory archives' which document certain traumatic experiences in the present which infiltrate into the present body politics. Here, the unique emotive function of war memorials may be noted. Recounting such excruciating experiences through disparate narratives has a therapeutic effect upon the authors; to them, writing helps heal the wounds, but the paradox is that such a very act gape opens the social wounds which refuse to heal themselves, making the present generation restless and sometimes guilty with its appeal to social conscience. Traumatic experiences of the dead are translated into the living generation, extending the former's 'after-life 'even more poignant. In *Unclaimed Experience*, Caruth rightly opines, "trauma is never simply one's own," and that "we are implicated in each other's trauma" (24).

Among the different aspects of cultural trauma studies, the question of agency is significant and it is important to observe who narrates the traumatic experiences. 'I,' the narrator, can be a witness and an empathiser. Here, we can see the infiltration of individual memory into the public domain, which eventually critiques mainstream discourses. In fact, such subversive narratives contain the tone of resistance and protest. In *Memories of a Father* by Echara Varier, for instance, the haunting memories of a son are recounted by the traumatised self of a father through the form of a memoir, and the narrative acts as a counter-discourse against the ruthless power structure. However, "the memoirist's narrative has the weight of authenticity and he puts the state on trial through his narrative, by speaking justice; perhaps even by knowing the fact that he was fighting a losing battle, Varier craves more of a divine justice" (Nair 893). Secondly, one can see the denial of agency where dehumanised, de-centred subjectivities are narrated. Gendered trauma further complicates the matter with its double victimisation, both by state and patriarchy. In T. D. Ramakrishnan's *Sugandhi Enna Andal Devanayaki* (2014), the official history of Sri Lanka is rewritten by exposing the brutal human rights violations against the Tamil immigrants, especially the plight of women including Rajani Thiranangama, Gayatri, Poomani, and Sugandhi by the fascist regime during the bloody civil war. Thus, through the novel T. D. Ramakrishnan

> tries to rewrite the social memory of Sri Lanka by attacking all sorts of domination whether it is by the Tigers or the Sri Lankan government. Fascism has no boundaries and the hegemonic public memory is deconstructed by the author by a violent counter-memory and an alternative one from the side of the dispossessed. (Nair63)

Obviously, there is politics of representation in such writings, which finally turn out to be counter-hegemonic narratives, attacking all power structures, including the state and patriarchy. One may not ignore the possibility of constructing spaces of sub-nationalism through such texts.

While studying traumatic experiences, we often commit the mistake of 'universalising' them, ignoring each one's uniqueness and heterogeneity. This becomes particularly relevant in the case of South Asia, where we come across a bewildering variety of sites of trauma, ranging from partition, emergency, to the Sri Lankan civil war. 'Gaps' and 'silences' are part and parcel of trauma narratives as many voices are deliberately obfuscated and marginalised. It may happen in the case of minorities, women, and other marginalised sections of society. The dominant/official version of the state subsumes other voices. Narratives of trauma offer resistance and protest against such hegemonic discourses. The plight of Sri Lankan Tamil migrants is represented through documentaries, films, literature, etc. Here, one can see the politics of representation where personal becomes political. Trauma narratives ultimately reconfigure the spaces through their voices of dissent. New spaces are redrawn and sometimes, we encounter what Lefebvre says, 'counter-spaces' or what Foucault calls 'heterotopias.'

Literature has its obvious limitations in representing trauma, but as a form, the graphic novel has its unique advantages – visuals can communicate more, apart from the speech balloons; silent panels with their colour combinations and shapes too, can communicate more. Trauma sites such as partition, emergency, Sri Lankan civil war, and gender atrocities have been adequately represented through graphic narratives in recent times in works such as Vishwajyoti Ghosh's edited anthology *This Side That Side* (2013), *Delhi Calm* (2010), Sarnath Banerjee's *Corridor* (2004), and *Drawing the Line: Indian Women Fight Back* (2015), a comics anthology edited by Larissa Bertonasco, Priya Kuriyan, and Ludmilla Bartscht. "Asha Now," in *Drawing the Line*, is Hemavathy Guha's story about a girl who is molested by her brother. It reminds us that a woman is not safe even within the four walls of her own home and family. The resultant trauma has a profound impact on her family life when she becomes a wife later, and Asha now is suspicious of everyone and feels insecure on behalf of her daughter when she is in the company of her uncle. Therefore, we need to study how trauma is narrated in graphic narratives because of its special attributes of verbal as well as visual modes of telling which complement each other.

In trauma narratives, the body becomes a powerful signifier, a site of multiple discourses. Violence is inflicted on the human body by the power structure to discipline and control it. In the case of Varier's memoir of his son as well as Ramakrishnan's novel, we witness scenes of brutal bodily violence inflicted by the state. In contrast, interestingly, sometimes the same body is used as a weapon against the state and we see women acting as suicide bombs, targeting the Sri Lankan President. Rajan's 'disappeared' body in the memoir appeals to the conscience of people and questions the repressive state apparatus. Among the various sites of trauma in South Asia, the Endosulfan incident in the Kasaragod district of Kerala deserves special mention. A large number of inhabitants in the northern district of Kerala have been suffering from trauma due to the frivolous, aerial spraying of pesticide on cashew plantations there. Many survivors are physically disabled and children, as well as women, are passing through mental agony. Many narratives, including novels such as AmbikasuthanMangad's*Enmakaje* (2009), memoirs such as Leelakumari Amma's *Jeevadayini* (2012), and penetrating photos by Madhuraj, document the excruciating, unspeakable trauma of the endosulfan victims. Visual texts communicate trauma more poignantly and the trauma faced by women and children is beautifully captured by the images of Madhuraj.

Source: madhurajsnaps.com

Photographs generate an "illusion of continuity over time and space" (Hirsch xi). They leave traces of the past, and obviously, bring back those who are dead, and hence, Sontag rightly calls photography "an elegiac art" (11), which evokes a sense of loss and pathos. She argues:"... all photographs are memento mori. To take a photograph is to participate in another person's (or thing's) mortality, vulnerability, mutability. Precisely by slicing out this moment and freezing it, all photographs testify to time's relentless melt" (11). They document evidences for the future. In *Camera Lucida* (1981), Barthes comments on this aspect: "...The important thing is that the photograph possesses an evidential force and that its testimony bears not on the object but on time. From a phenomenological viewpoint, in the photograph, the power of authentication exceeds the power of representation" (88-89).

Memory is a narrative construct and it offers an alternative interpretation of an event. History may also be considered as an employment of events (White 1973), if not full of facts. Traumatic incidents reflect scenes of strife in narrating memories. Homi Bhabha calls them revisionary narratives as they openly challenge the mainstream discourses of a nation, including the notion of a welfare state; they also question the very existence of a nation-state (1990). They are scars on the body politic. Such writings on trauma help in remapping a nation-state with its underlying tone of fear and sometimes dissent. In fact, trauma indicates a denial of subjectivity and agency. Recalcitrant, dissenting subjects come under the surveillance of the state and they are often targeted, punished, and disciplined by several mechanisms of torture. Political subjectivity is ensured and emphasised, and disloyalty is an anathema that cannot be excused under any circumstances. Hence, we encounter an increase in the number of homosacers in our society. Thus, the sovereignty of the state is privileged over the human rights of citizens. We may also view them as minority narratives exposing the fissures and conflicts within dominant nation-states. Writing becomes a process of archiving memories, providing afterlives for the victims. Are these narratives taken as 'counter narratives?' To a certain extent, yes, because they problematise the notion of nation and its logic, challenging the official, hegemonic versions of history, as they expose the possibilities of alternative voices and spaces.

The narratives discussed above have unequivocally highlighted the issue of human rights and emphasised that writing/documenting such experiences is a matter of righting wrongs by appealing to human conscience, particularly in this age of surveillance. As a matter of fact, fear is an underlying emotion underpinning these works, and it is a matter of concern how far dissent is welcomed in the current political atmosphere in South Asia. When it comes to 'reading' as an act, I would reckon it as a political act. Decoding trauma in such writings is a matter of identification with the victims. In a wider context, do such readings help in remaking the mindset of civil society? Here, it may be added that including such texts as part of pedagogy (which already is) will go a long way towards making us more concerned about our fellow beings who struggle to wriggle themselves out of the vortex of traumatic events.

Recounting various horrific events in writing affects readers; the process itself is chilling but also healing and chastening. Writing reveals itself to be a social activity for chronicling unique traumatic experiences, and it is critical to examine how societal values are ascribed through it. Individuals get sensitised to such empathetic documents. However, we cannot ignore the dissenting and protesting aspects of such narratives because they invariably highlight all manner of flagrant human rights violations and atrocities occurring around us, appeal to social conscience, and occasionally call into question our indifference to hapless trauma victims. In this context, their works serve the noble function of exposing societal injustices and challenging social indifference.

Notes

1. Memories are represented through writings as well as material objects. It is important to notice that memory happens only after an event, and therefore, the 'constructedness' of it through narratives is important. Literature is a mnemonic act, and writing is both an act of memory and a new interpretation by which every new text is etched into memory space. In fact, literature is a storage medium for memories and one can see the transmission of knowledge in society through different narrative representations. In literary texts, we see only 'fictions of memory,' an imaginative reconstruction of the past where negotiation of cultural memory takes place amidst the never-ending conflicts between sanctioned and unsanctioned memories. Among the key theorists of memory studies, the name of Maurice Halbwachs is preeminent. It was he who introduced the notion of memoire collective (collective memory), and argued that personal memory is collective memory because individual memory is a creation of tradition, one dependent on social frameworks. Another theorist, Pierre Nora, in Realms of Memory connects memory with history and nation and introduces the concept of 'sites of memory.' Andreas Huyssen expands Nora's point and studies sites of memory from postcolonial, multicultural, diasporic, transcultural, and transnational perspectives. Aleida Assmann and Jan Assmann, the German theorists, approach memory by tying it with material objectivations. To them, memory is constituted by social groups with the help of a system of values.
2. Rajan, the son of T.V. Eachara Warrior, was a final year student at Calicut Engineering College, when he was taken into custody for his alleged involvement in Naxalite activities. As per official records, he was not arrested, but it is believed that Rajan was tortured to death in a camp by the police.
3. As a violent movement, Naxalism broke out in Kerala, drawing inspiration from the leadership of Charu Majumdar and Kanu Sanyal in the West Bengal state of India. In fact, naxals are communist revolutionaries who want social change through revolutionary means. However, naxalism failed to take root in Kerala after attacks such as Pulpally in Wynad, Kuttiyadi and Thirunelly in Kerala. In Kerala, Kunnikkal Ajitha was a prominent face in the movement during the 1960s and was notorious for armed raids on Thalassery and Pulpally police stations. Mandakini Narayanan or Ma, the mother of Ajitha, was also a naxalite leader in Kerala.

Works Cited

Assmann, Jan. "Collective Memory and Cultural Identity." *The Collective Memory Reader.* Olick, Jeffery K., et al. Cambridge UP, 2011.

Barthes, Roland. *Camera Lucida: Reflections on Photography.* Translated by Richard Howard, New York: Hill and Wang, 1981.

Bhabha, Homi. *Nation and Narration.* Routledge, 1990.

Caruth, Cathy. *Unclaimed Experience: Trauma, Narrative, and Memory.* The John Hopkins UP, 1996.

.... editor. *Trauma: Explorations in Memory.* The John Hopkins UP, 1995.

Connerton, Paul. *How Societies Remember.* New York: CUP, 1989.

Guha, Hemavathy. "Asha Now". *Drawing the Line:Indian Women Fight Back*, edited by Larissa Bertonasco, Ludmilla Bartscht and Priya Kuriyan.Zubaan Books, 2015.

Hirsch, Marianne. *Family Frames: Photography Narrative and Postmemory.* Cambridge: Harvard UP, 2012.

Lefebvre, Henri. *The Production of Space.* Blackwell Publishing, 1991.

Nair, Rajesh V. "Raising the Dead: Reframing Public Memory in T. V. Eachara Varier's Memoir Memories of a Father." *Literary Herald*, vol 3, no 1, 2017.

..........*Critical Musings: Essays on Literature and Culture.* Green Books, 2016.

Ramakrishnan, T.D. *Sugandhi Enna Andal Devanayaki.* D C Books, 2014.

Sontag, Susan. *On Photography.* St. Martin's P, 1977.

Varier, Eachara. *Memories of a Father.* Trans. Neelan. Asian Human Rights Commission, 2004.

White, Hayden. *Metahistory: The Historical Imagination in Nineteenth Century Europe.* John Hopkins UP, 1973.

CHAPTER 4

Transmission of Trauma in Dystopian Fiction: A Study of Margaret Atwood's *The Handmaid's Tale* and *The Testaments*

Joji John Panicker

Literature as a Mirror to Life and Trauma

Literature is the aesthetic human expression which mirrors life, society and its changes. The changes in life and society influenced and prompted writers to describe, warn and predict generations of their truth and future. "The relationship between literature and society is far more subtle and complex than social scientists or cultural critics commonly assume" (Glicksberg 1). Every literary work or artistic expression reflects the pressures, desires, tensions, confusions, fears, aspirations and logic of that age. "Obviously literature does not operate in a vacuum: it is pre-eminently a social act as a social product" (1).

The value norms and ethics portrayed in literature often induce people to pause and reflect on their own actions and behaviours. Consciously or unconsciously, literature influences the complex psyche of human beings and the dynamics of society. "The purpose of literature as magic is to arouse emotions or reactions which can then be deflected into channels of socio-political reform" (Glicksberg 8). Literature empowers writers to display the interior and most private world of the human mind. The deep cauldron of reminiscences, perception, introspection, augurs, flashback and recollections and commemorations inside each and every individual tinted with wound, pain and subsequent trauma has found its path to literature for centuries.

Trauma, the term refers to a state or human condition which is the repercussion of a profound and unfathomable injury or affliction. Freud in *Beyond Pleasure Principle* defined traumatic neurosis as "a consequence of an extensive breach being made in the protective shield against stimuli" (303). The disturbing and destructive experience of individual creates a profound impact on the conscious and unconscious realm of the human mind. Literature uses language to convey inner trauma. "First trauma was mainly associated with extremely unusual events; it has now become a powerful and complex paradigm that infiltrates contemporary history, literature, culture and critical theory" (Nadal1). According to many prominent theorists, "ours appears to be the age of trauma" (Miller 1) and literature paints this "catastrophic age" (Caruth 11) in the most vivid and effective way. The portrayal of trauma of characters in the literary arena gives the space to contemplate and be "responsive to the traumatic experience of others" (LaCapra 41).

The literature concerning the Holocaust and other great catastrophes like the World Wars conveys the trauma of the age and the experience. Literary and non-literary works like *Night* by Elie Wiesel, *Diary of a Young Girl* by Anne Frank, *If This Is a Man* by Primo Levi, *The Reader* by Bernhard Schlink, *A Farewell to Arms* by Ernest Hemingway and *Poems of Wilfred Owen* by Wilfred Owen portray the dreadful experience of inscrutable and incomprehensible episodes of history. The real and imaginative characters of these literary representations reveal the trauma of being tangled in an uncontrollable convulsion of outrageous happenings. The expression and exploration of trauma in literary expression paved the way for an advanced analysis of literary works on the basis of trauma. Explication of psychoanalytic studies influenced and impacted literary theories and theorists.

Trauma theory developed in the 1990s in connection with the ethical turn that emerged in the previous decade and which affected literary theory and philosophy. In different manners, the increasing interest in trauma was a response to concerns about memory, the politics, representation and ethics that became prominent at the turn of the twentieth century, and which have mainly focused on the extreme forms of violence and victimisation that came to light after World War II (Nadal 1).

Besides Holocaust and World War narratives of all kinds, trauma is very much underlined in fiction depicting environments which oppress and humiliate; where the characters are trapped in dystopian regimes of megalomaniacs. Reality is often stranger than fiction; the fictional world and characters represent the reality in an emblematic way, thus informing us about our own surroundings and reality, because "post humanist depictions of trauma can disturb readers into an ethic of radical openness and vulnerability" (Vinci 2014 93). Oppression, humiliation and injustice gives rise to trauma and this aspect of human psyche needs to be studied. Prolonged exposure to discrimination and tyranny can either corrode the identity of the individual or can provoke the person into retaliating against the oppressive circumstances. Trauma and survival, both are crucial for the evolution of the individual to the next level.

Trauma narratives reveal the innate literariness of the traumatic experience; thus, non-realist texts that experiment with modernist and postmodernist techniques in an effort to destabilise coherent notions of the world and subjectivity via fragmentation, stream of consciousness, flattening of affect, non-linear narrative structures, and so on become the dominant locus of study for classic trauma theorists (Vinci 2020).

Literature expresses trauma and the effects of its repression on characters or individuals thus touching upon the strictly private aspects of the human mind. Given that the genre of novels deals primarily with the individuals' struggles in different environments, it can pertinently portray the psyche of individual characters, how they deal with different levels of trauma and how they try to survive the trauma inflicted by their surroundings. Novel, as a genre, facilitates a poignancy and propinquity of expression when dealing with trauma. Trauma narratives depict individual experiences of trauma and survival, and at the same time, arbitrate on the nature of collective trauma imposed by socio-cultural and political prejudices and subjugation.

Trauma: An Overview

The dialectics of trauma is complex in that both the victims and witnesses suffer. Trauma can be the result of a single sudden frightful or life-threatening event or a prolonged experience that systematically subjugates and routs an individual's psyche. The overwhelming stress and oppression surpass one's ability to deal with the powerful emotions associated with an intimidating experience. Study of trauma has its origins in clinical psychology. Trauma can be the after-effect of sexual abuse, employment bigotry, police cruelty, harassment, marital violence, and mostly childhood experience. Past traumatic experiences and its memories can affect the psyche of the victim in varied ways. Different people react differently to the same traumatic incident, and in consequence of their subjective experiences of trauma. Not all individuals become traumatised by the same event.

Response to trauma may vary according to the subjective psychology of the individuals. Troubling emotions such as panic, exasperation, guilt, indignity, feeling of helplessness and vulnerability are manifested in myriad forms. With respect to individual differences, idiosyncratic encountering of the traumatic experiences, create discrepancy which can be noted in the reaction to corresponding events. Root causes of traumatic experiences encompass intimidation, humiliation, desertion, rejection, deception among others which habitually places the individual in a state of indecision and insecurity. Implicit memories of trauma might not be voiced but actuated by experiences encircling the victim. Trauma involves not just unfathomable personal suffering, but also a sincere struggle to cope with the realities.

Cathy Caruth's *Unclaimed Experience: Trauma, Narrative and History* is considered as one of the pioneering works in the discipline of trauma. Caruth resists the term trauma studies and claims that the phrasing "has the disadvantage of codifying the term trauma and eliminating some of its surprise and literariness" (174). Caruth insists on the ethical significance of this critical practice. She claims that "the language of trauma, and the silence of its mute repetition of suffering, profoundly and imperatively demand a new mode of reading and of listening" (9).

With publications of Cathy Caruth's work and Kali Tal's *World's Hart, Reading the Literature of Trauma*, trauma studies obtained notable scrutiny in the field of literary criticism. According to Caruth, the pioneer of psychoanalytic post structural approach, inherent contradiction of language and experience was explicated through the trauma which is an untold problem of the unconscious. Caruth considers literature and trauma as intensely connected. The theory potentially derived from her insightful explication and expatiation of Freud's deliberations on traumatic experiences in *Beyond the Pleasure Principle* and *Moses and Monotheism.* While her account of trauma demonstrates Freud's influence, Caruth secured her literary theory determinedly to the work of modern clinical trauma experts, most importantly Bessel van der Kolk and Judith Herman. The two most significant fundamental tenets of her representation of trauma are its amnesic feature and its unspeakability. Caruth's arguments that trauma is sometimes almost if not completely unspeakable, the thought which she developed in her analysis of Freud in *Unclaimed Experience*, was reinforced by the points of view of van der Kolk and Herman.

According to Caruth, the traumatic experience is unclaimed and in trauma, the terrible incident appears with such life changing force that it scuttles the brain's function, and the victim is incapable of comprehending the occurrence in a standard way. Trauma compels the identity into hiding, and though the various senses keep in contact and records sights, sounds, smells, and feelings, the brain fails to work them through. The videographer leaves, but the tape keeps running. The trauma, then, is "an event whose force is marked by its lack of registration" (Caruth6) and traumatic memories are so complex and varied it insists on being told, although the explication can be fragmented, non-linear and abstract.

Public and professional thoughtfulness towards the tribulations connected with trauma had developed considerably in the earlier years. Currently, the interdisciplinary approach to the study of trauma is in great vogue; as it is closely associated with further disciplines such as psychology, sociology, history, politics and principally literature.

As the science of trauma changed over the past years, the literary theory of trauma has also had significant changes. Theories, on which Caruth depends, have been confronted and challenged in the recent years with current clinical studies of the psychology of trauma. Richard McNally of Harvard issued a review of a recent research in 2003 that has been broadly observed as a warning to trauma studies starting to change. Unlike Caruth, McNally argues that trauma is unforgettable and describable; his works take up important questions about the clinical foundation on which Caruth constructs her literary structure and paradigm, necessitating modern critics to reconsider and reassess her model. McNally also rejects the notion and ideas about the implication that traumatic memory cannot be uttered or expressed in words. He permits and entertains the thought that the memory of trauma may be distorted, but he discards the idea that it is deficient and absent: "[P]eople who have experienced harrowingly close brushes with death (such as falling off a mountain) often report extreme dissociative alterations of consciousness (time slowing down, everything seeming unreal), yet they remain fully capable of providing detailed accounts of their experiences" (182).

Transgenerational Quality of Trauma

The transmission of trauma and survival mechanisms from one generation to the next, sometimes succeeding generations as well, is called transgenerational trauma. In the bigger realm of trauma studies, the field of trauma transmission studies shot to prominence in the 1970s with the huge exploration and analysis of trauma and torment in the family dynamics of second-generation Holocaust survivors. Those who had been brought up with, and had psychically taken in the Holocaust trauma, as well as the parental generation that met what Lacan calls, the Real and the catastrophic event which distorted the form of human account everlastingly, are the embodiment of trauma. To defend against the dissociation of that tradition and to bring its full, catastrophic tale into social dialogue might be the one mission of transmission of trauma.

The analysis of the features of the Holocaust history and experiences, especially, through the experiences of the children of those who survived the traumatic event, gave ground for the original arena of trauma transmission studies or transgenerational trauma studies. Those children of second generation who intensely recognise with their parents' heritage, tradition, wounds and related trauma, also seem to partake in their parents' suffering and pain, which the outside world forcefully ingrained in them.

The children of survivors frequently conveyed and were engrossed by the wounds, pain and trauma associated with the Holocaust. The psychoanalytic literature on the children of Holocaust survivors proves that the Holocaust is imprinted on them through early, unconscious identifications. The children of the survivors consciously or unconsciously exhibit the trauma of their parents – the pain, suffering, and survival strategies are passed on to them as a tradition. Trauma which has been inherited from the events, caused by a single instant in time, single moment in history, resurfaces over the years with a new meaning. Episodes such as the Holocaust persist to carry to our approach, novel traditions to explore trauma, across generations, in dissimilar fractions of the world, over a period of more than sixty years. Inner transformations and subjective perspectives, which are the result of way of living and changes in the environment, can influence the course and authority of trauma's transmission.

The classic Freudian definition of trauma, two generations ago, was that it was powerless, incapable, and fruitless. Now it is considered self-assured, capable of preservation, and those suffering are deemed competent enough to work out choices of self-protection; not only the preservation but also the transmission of the competencies has been broached. Experimental work, offer a privileged window to the nature, mechanisms, and consequences of the transmission of trauma: its horror, intimacy, and uncanny re-emergence in the transference particularly in the unconscious material, relational dynamics, and emotional interactions of deep detail psychotherapy.

Transmission of trauma gives the impression that it employs an unconscious trail; Freud spoke about unconscious connections and associations between people; the transmission of trauma appears to use this unconscious channel, between parent and child and between patient and therapist. Freud in his extraordinary, unexplained, and totally outright statement says that "everyone possesses in his own unconscious an instrument with which he can interpret the utterances of the unconscious in other people" (320). As a matter of fact, it was the query of trauma that steered Freud to a re-examination of the ego and its workings in *Beyond the Pleasure Principle*; this re-examination was a consequence of his encounter with the psychologically wounded of the First World War.

In the past years trauma studies have proliferated and encouraged experimental research to broader realms rather than remaining on slender focal point on post-traumatic stress disorder to a wider admiration of conditions of tremendous stimulation, both unexpected and continued, in which the adaptive surviving devices of a person shut down in favour of enormous dissociation. The handing down of trauma from one generation to the next takes on various guises. For example, anxiety or other sentiments could be passed from parent to child. Or unconscious fantasies about the reason, character, and reverberations of the trauma might be passed on. Sometimes an unconscious mission is imparted to the child, for example, to take revenge for a parent's dishonor or to make up for an awful failure. Experimental experience conducted by Austen Riggs regarding Holocaust studies demonstrates that the possessions of trauma are carried ahead, not only into the subsequent generation, but also into the succeeding generations and conceivably ensuing generations as well.

Inside this transmission, there is an inconsistency that can be traced; which is silence, silence is a persistent feature in the transmission of trauma, silence about something both awfully perplexing and completely imperative. This silence about trauma may or may not get diluted in the succeeding generations. The unspeakability of one generation's trauma gets transmitted differently to the next generation. It speaks and informs the succeeding generation in dissimilar ways. The communication of the first generation to the next generation regarding trauma and survival with descriptions, instill the next generation with affect-laden stimulus.

Frequent talks about the unnamed something in the family legacy is passed on to the next generation. Recurring jokes and wordplay between family members frequently conserve in custom form, a bit of family trauma, something related to the traumatic event that is unrelenting and concomitantly renounced. The unnamed traumatic legacy remains indistinct and accordingly potentially ubiquitous. The next generation to which this legacy is passed will take the account with full seriousness and confidentiality of pain that the first generation has undergone. And this perpetuation of faith to the succeeding generations is conspicuous and mystifying.

Researchers Danieli, Katz and Kellermann have claimed that the transmission of trauma was arbitrated by the lack of open and deep communication and conveyance about the bygone and the emotional withdrawal which was thought to characterise the survivor parent, and the transmission of trauma was seen as a result of unconscious relocated sentiments and emotions. Many authors still seem to take the early conclusions regarding the unspeakability for granted, although there have been astonishingly few studies in which communication patterns regarding transmission of trauma within non-Western refugee populations are explored empirically. To address the debate concerning disclosure versus silencing of trauma many attempts are being conducted including the analysis of traumatic experiences from the past on the mental health, psychosocial adjustment, and wellbeing of children of refugee parents.

Tracing Trauma: *The Handmaid's Tale* and *The Testaments*

The Handmaid's Tale by Margaret Atwood is a novel which portrays the trauma that accumulates in different sections of a society which is totalitarian and dystopian in nature.

The trauma caused to the characters due to the systematic oppression, social hierarchy, the loss of freedom, sexual and physical exploitation and the convoluted technicalities of terror are the major concern of the novel. Offred's forbidden relationship with the household's guardian is an act of rebellion against this totalitarian structure. The role of women in The Republic of Gilead as child bearers and housekeepers conforms to the traditional patriarchal notions. The portrayal of power as a perversion of human potential and the resultant trauma it causes to those in the margins is depicted in detail.

Healthy women of the Republic of Gilead are trained with totalitarian ideology and forced into sexual slavery. The sexual slavery named as Ceremony, which creates physical and mental trauma to the handmaids forces them into silence and further annihilation. It is not just the handmaids that are exploited, all the citizens of Gilead are forced to live a life based on "frugality, conformity, censorship, corruption, fear, and terror" (Malak 10) which force them into trauma and further consequences as none of this distress and sufferings are taken into consideration. The oppressing social hierarchy consists of numerous functional structures such as hand maids and Commanders of the Faithful.

Every individual in the Republic of Gilead has their own function; the Unwomen and the Econowives are the two groups of women who are not divided according to function who also undergo trauma. Even though these two factions do not have any official purposes, they are an essential fraction of the oppressive societal configuration. Handmaids are indoctrinated to believe that if they do not follow the existing rules, they will be exiled and exterminated.

The profound and constant pressure of being made to procreate makes the handmaids suffer continuous tension and mental torture. Besides the physical torment, the emotional trauma of being used as a material for child bearing ensure that the handmaids endure individual as well as collective trauma. The community trauma of handmaids is shared and sustained among them. The shared trauma offered them ways to with deal it, sometimes it is silence and self-annihilation, other times it is the desire to break way by small rebellion. The trauma forces them to rebel in their own private ways, not in the most reflective and philosophical manner. The invariable intimidation of being confirmed as the Unwomen and thrown into the Colonies is the constant trauma under which the handmaids reside. They are no longer of any use to the society if they are unsuccessful in producing the progeny even at their third redistribution.

In the Republic, Marthas the women who do the menial jobs like cooking, cleaning, and taking care of the household in general are considered to be at the bottom of the societal structure. Because of their incapability to bear children, they are considered less valuable and deprived of the right to marry. They are forced into a life of physical slavery where they have to bear the trauma of being treated as worthless in the society. All the people in the society are dressed according to their social status according to the government rule. Marthas wear dull green dresses, "like a surgeon's gown of the time before" (Atwood 9) and have more freedom regarding their public appearance. He handmaids are allowed a certain dress code and are not allowed to show their face. Offred describes the appearance of Rita, a Martha who works in the same household: "The 8 dresses is much like mine in shape, long and concealing, but with a bib apron over it and without the white wings and the veil. She puts the veil to go outside, but nobody much cares who sees the face of a Martha" (9). Apart from the women who are treated as objects for physical and sexual use, the men in the lower strata of the society also tolerate significant oppression and trauma due to injustice, tyranny and subjugation. The Guardians who serve their masters, the Commanders, belong to the lower place in the oppressive regime. Their primary job is security of the Commanders and their wives and daughters. As Offred describes, "The Guardians aren't real soldiers. They're used for routine policing and other menial functions, digging up the Commander's Wife's garden, for instance, and they're either stupid or older or disabled or very young ..." (20). The only groups of people, who belong to the secondary strata in this novel who enjoy power to a certain amount, are the Aunts. Like their name implies, they embody a moderately respected figure and their major duty is to mould the handmaids for their procreative functions. The function of Aunts represents the perfect example of how systematic oppression and resultant trauma occurs. Human beings have been dispossessed of their independence and trained to perform according to their societal rank.

The Testaments, the sequel to *The Handmaid's Tale*, portrays the final years of the Gilead. The totalitarian regime depicted in the novel describes the power and potential of oppressive structures already realised in history. Gilead being a totalitarian regime uses religion as a tool to suppress and oppress citizens in the margin. Intending to subjugate women furthermore, the marital structure is based on Abraham's life in the *Old Testament*, thus propagating regressive views regarding women and their role. Those in power take advantage of women and induce trauma. The male leadership of the regime is repressing women's sexuality and uses their power to satisfy their violent and often pedophilic fantasies. The trauma of the victims of this lecherous sexual violence forces them to rebel.

The narrative of Agnes, which depicts her life in primary school through beginning of adulthood, shows the length and depth of indoctrination, brutal punishment and the fear instilled in her by using her own sexuality. And as Becka says "the goal in every instance was the same: girls of all kinds – those from good families as well as the less favored – were to be married early, before any chance encounter with an unsuitable man might occur that would lead to what used to be called falling in love or, worse, to loss of virginity" (Atwood 154). The regime makes female sexuality a tool to make them fear recognising and exploring their sexuality, thus controlling and subjugating them. They are taught lessons like "But if we were to put too much emphasis on the theoretical delights of sex, the result would almost certainly be curiosity and experimentation, followed by moral degeneracy and public stoning" (214). The trauma of being under constant supervision and threat of being excluded create havoc on the psyche of individuals. Agnes's experience showcases how repressive regimes make use of fear and shame to repress one's sexuality and identity thus making them submissive.

Even as child, individuals are taught to fear their sexuality if one of them gets forcibly violated, it is their fault. In the novel Agnes has nightmares of this indoctrination which traumatises her. The trauma of being beneath such constant threat of being violated is psychologically damaging. When Agnes reaches adulthood, she becomes more and more afraid of her body and considers herself better off without it. The changes in her body create a sense of panic and terror in her that it causes additional fear and trauma which finally manifests as self-contempt. The societal and community trauma related to female sexuality and the oppression of it, is shared by all the women in the regime. Denial of justice and fear create trauma and fear of the punishment of public shaming. The stigma, shame and ensuing trauma pervades every aspect of the society. Girls are forced to marry by their first menstruation, the immense pressure and stress of conforming to strict gender roles. Becka and Agnes fear their impending forced marriage and are traumatised by the thought of having sex with their much older husbands. This trauma even forces them to try to annihilate themselves. "[Becka] really did believe that marriage would obliterate her. She would be crushed, she would be nullified, she would be melted like snow until nothing remained of her" (163).

Women have to be silent about abuse and the consequential trauma forces them into a space of an under developed sense of self. The silence and trauma inhibits them from standing up for themselves. The trauma of suppressing the intellectual and physical potentials drives them crazy and forces them to fight back in any way they could. The lack of choice and autonomy becomes the source of anger, frustration, fear and trauma for Agnes and Becka. The Ofkyle's death creates shock in Becka, which showcases the lack of choice and freedom individuals have. Becka's suicide signifies what she considers will be her final option in the face of a choiceless life, a marital existence devoid of agency.

The Testaments portrays the concept of choice and agency as a multifaceted concern: choice is a significant human right and it is an injustice when one's choice and agency are deprived. This trauma can either force them into silence and self-annihilation due to the indoctrination or it forces them to fight back.

Tracing the Transgenerational Trauma

As trauma and related survival mechanisms can be passed down to the subsequent generations. The oppression and related trauma portrayed in the individual and collective space of characters in *The Handmaid's Tale* can be traced to *The Testaments*. Both the novels chronicle life and survival in the Republic of Gilead. The events in *The Testaments* occur fifteen years after the incidents portrayed in *The Handmaid's Tale*.

The tale of Offred is an imaginary one, but this fiction has an uncanny resemblance to reality as it is filled with real crimes against humanity. The atrocities depicted in the novel propels trauma. The world of *The Handmaid's Tale* is so totalitarian that it induces trauma in every single character that is not privileged. The sequel also depicts the same disturbingly believable dystopian world and the trauma of the previous generation, on individual, collective and societal levels which gets transmitted to the next generation. The world of Gilead has not changed much; the indoctrination continues to oppress and mould people for the benefit of those who are in power. The transmitted trauma at individual and collective levels prompt some to think that there is no way out while others with their acquired knowledge and companionship revolt and fight back. The knowledge of the stimulated trauma impels some to act and save others.

The transmission of trauma from one generation of handmaids to the next is depicted in the first novel. The protagonist of *The Handmaid's Tale* is nameless throughout the tale. The oppression and constant suppression makes her submissive and even traumatised to the extent where she is rebellious and even violent in her thoughts. The communal trauma of constant supervision and brutal indoctrination impels psychological trauma in the handmaids which they share and transmit over generations. Although the initial generations silently succumbed to trauma and death the Next generations of handmaids inherited not only the trauma but also the rebellious streak. The need and desire to escape from the trauma forces them to act, silently and also secretively. The honest emotions and keen observation of Offred illustrates her private revolts and her inner desire to survive.

The character of Janine or Of warren showcases the extreme trauma of women in the regime; she becomes hysterical; and criticised and broken at the Rachel and Leah Center. The previous handmaid, who Offred never meets, conveys her anger, frustration and trauma to Offred through her scratching in the closet. The unnamed previous handmaid hanged herself in the house. The suicide portrays the trauma and frustration she had, she speaks or sparks the rebellion she wanted but could not practice. The handmaid in the sequel is Ofkyle, who is ignored by everyone until she gets pregnant. When she gets pregnant, it is her womb that is being taken care of. She is reduced to only her womb. The identity and self of Ofkyle is demeaned and dehumanised by everyone who admires her pregnant belly. And finally, she is killed during her delivery. Ofkyle never had any choice in the matter regarding sacrificing herself for the child. This incident instigates a huge shock, realisation and trauma in Agnes. The lack of choice over one's life and health traumatises the women. The problems faced by the handmaids remain the same but they try to identify themselves and their desires in the subsequent generations. The pain, suffering and trauma of previous generation are transmitted to the next generation; at the same time the revolts and survival strategies are also passed down.

The trauma transmitted from one generation of mothers to the next generation is evident in the relationship between Offred and her mother, and Ada's constant watch over Nicole. The relationship between Offred and her mother is strained, her mother's end in the Colonies traumatises Offred and she regrets about their difficult relationship. The trauma of being separated from one's child is experienced by every handmaid in the regime. The transmission of trauma from comrade to comrade can be traced in the two books. Trauma of being subjugated forces them to break away from the oppressing system. They try to run away from the oppression. The underprivileged in the totalitarian society form a union in opposition to the systematic tyranny. The secret actions of Aunt Lydia showcase the trauma she bears due to her role in the building of Gilead. She saves girls by making them aunts and orchestrates their escape to Canada; she also passes secret information to the Mayday resistance operation.

The societal trauma that women feel under the regime is passed down from generation to generation. The teaching and the training given to women in the regime; force them to regard themselves as un-intellectual creatures of inferiority. The trauma of being inferior in every aspect forces them to be silent about the abuse they have to suffer. Becka's father sexually abuses many girls including Becka and Agnes. They refuse to speak out because of the inferiority they feel about themselves as well as the shame they feel in revealing the incidents in public. Both the girls contemplate death rather than marrying without their consent. This shows the extent of trauma they suffer. The individual trauma experience and the collective trauma shared by characters in the novels showcase the transmission of it through generations. It is not just trauma that is transmitted but the flickers of personal revolts too are handed down which culminates in the fall of Gilead.

Conclusion

Transgenerational trauma is the collective emotional and psychological wounding that is transmitted from one generation to the subsequent generation. Violent past events, bigotry, and tyranny experienced by previous generations can potentially influence the lives of upcoming generations in the form of unsettled anguish and continuing trauma. The consequences of these collective traumas continue to be apparent in the behaviors of the individual experiencing the trauma similar to the previous generation; it is not just the trauma that is manifested in subsequent generations but also the waves of resistance and the survival techniques.

Atwood's *The Handmaid's Tale* and *The Testaments*, both chronicle the tale of oppression and defiance in the dystopian Republic of Gilead. The trauma of the under privileged, especially the women in different strata of the society is transmitted to the next generation. The sparks of resistance and secret survival techniques are also transmitted. The physical, sexual, emotional wounds, pain, suffering and related trauma induce silence as well as resistance which is passed down passively and actively. The indoctrination of passivity and submission initiates intellectual and physical trauma in the people of Gilead.

The life of the handmaids is miserable. The handmaid, who lived in the house before Offred, took her life as an act of defiance against the restricting regime. Her defiance also extended to her scratching of "Nolitetebastardescarborundorum" (Atwood 52) at the bottom of the cupboard. Offred acknowledges this scratched message as a testimony that the handmaids are not completely helpless. Even a minute act of rebellion is better than absolute passivity and tameness. Alike Offred, several characters are recipients of the trauma, the defiance and the resistance handed down from their previous generations of handmaids which ultimately empower them to bring down the oppressive regime of Gilead in their own secretive and guarded way. Transgenerational trauma can be a persuasive and effective agency of resistance, revolt and emancipation in a world of tyrannical and exploitive environment. This agency can pass on to the next generation and empower them to fight against the oppressive system.

Works cited

Atwood, Margaret. *The Handmaid's Tale*. London: Vintage, 1996.

..........*The Testaments.* Thorpe, Charnwood, 2020.

Caruth, Cathy. *Trauma: Explorations in Memory.* Johns Hopkins UP, 1995.

.... *Unclaimed Experience: Trauma, Narrative, and History.* Johns Hopkins UP, 1996.

Danieli, Y. *International Handbook of Multigenerational Legacies of Trauma.* Springer, 1998.

Freud, Sigmund, et al. *Beyond the Pleasure Principle.* Broadview P, 2011.

.... "The Disposition to Obsessional Neurosis. A Contribution to the Problem of Choice of Neurosis (1913)." pp. 318-323. *PsycEXTRA Dataset,* 1971, doi:10.1037/e417472005-300.

Glicksberg, Charles I. *Literature and Society.* Nijhoff, 1972.

Katz, M. "Prisoners of Azkaban: Understanding intergenerational transmission of trauma due to war and state terror (with help from Harry Potter)". *Journal for the Psychoanalysis of Culture and Society*, vol. 8, no. 2, 2003, pp. 200-207.

Kellerman, N. P. "Psychopathology in children of Holocaust survivors: a review of the research literature". *Israel Journal of Psychiatry and Related Sciences*, 2001. pp. 38.

LaCapra, Dominick. *Writing History, Writing Trauma.* Johns Hopkins UP, 2014.

Malak, Amin. "Margaret Atwood's The Handmaid's Tale and the Dystopian Tradition." *Canadian Literature*, 1987, pp. 9-16.

McNally, Richard J. *Remembering Trauma.* Harvard UP, 2003

Miller, Nancy K., and Jason Tougaw. *Extremities: Trauma, Testimony, and Community.* U of Illinois P, 2002.

Nadal, Marita, and Mónica Calvo. *Trauma in Contemporary Literature: Narrative and Representation.* Routledge Taylor & Francis Group, 2014.

Vinci, Tony M. *Ghost, Android, Animal: Trauma and Literature beyond the Human.* Routledge, 2020. Google Books, bit.ly/3m6Avi3. Accessed 6 June 2020.

.... "Posthuman Wounds: Trauma, Non-Anthropocentric Vulnerability, and the Human/Android/Animal Dynamic in Philip K. Dick's 'Do Androids Dream of Electric Sheep?" *The Journal of the Midwest Modern Language Association,* vol. 47, no. 2, Midwest Modern Language Association, 2014, pp. 91-112.

CHAPTER 5

Trans-generational Transmission of Collective Trauma and Memory: A Reading of Leila Abdelrazaq's *Baddawi*

Kochurani Joseph

Trauma is an unspeakable experience that thwarts the physical, emotional and mental balance of an individual. It is a lifelong scar that a traumatic event leaves on the memory and psyche. Studies on trauma usually analyse the effects of the event on the particular individual. However traumatic events do not always get limited to an individual or a generation in their impact.

According to Elizabeth Batista and Pinto Wiese, trauma is to be measured within a culture, because the cultural context shapes all the life experiences including the traumatic ones (142-152). In the opinion of Nigel Rapport and Joanna Overing culture consists of "elements which are defined and differentiated in a particular society as representing reality – the total reality of life within which human beings live and die" (95). Culture is so vital that its deprivation makes the victim's thinking behaving and living outside a particular cultural system makes the whole existence abnormal, deviant, dysfunctional and meaningless. So "very often it is not the human bodies, but the world-view of a given collective that suffers in a collective trauma" (Aarelaid-Tart 43).

Sociologist Kai Erikson differentiates between individual and collective trauma and their influence on the individual self and community.

> By individual trauma I mean a blow to the psyche that breaks through one's defenses so suddenly and with such brutal force that one cannot react to it effectively…by collective trauma, on the other hand, I mean a

> blow to the basic tissues of social life that damages the bonds attaching people together and impairs the prevailing sense of communality (153).

He regards the progression of collective trauma as slow and its realisation, gradual on the understanding of the people who are to suffer from it. But through this steady process community falls apart and no longer offer effective support. He concludes the situation as deterioration of the self where "We no longer exist as a connected pair or as linked cells in a larger communal body" (154).

According to Arthur G. Neil, "Collective trauma is a volcanic disruption of everyday life" (9). Historical and collective trauma is a common experience for a group of people and their position and function in society. When historical upheavals shake the existing social systems and challenge the existence of its people to disrupt the flow of life, they undergo a cultural and historical trauma. Linda O'Neill and others argue that Historical trauma can affect generations upon generations until the trauma is ingrained into society as it causes a greater loss of identity and meaning for individuals and community (173-186). Collective trauma threatens collective identity. It questions the significance of the group and the wisdom of being part of a persecuted and humiliated crowd.

One group of people who are likely to experience this complex historical, cultural trauma is refugees. Refugees are "individuals forced to flee their countries of origin in the context of political violence, persecution, and instability" (Sangalang, et al. 2). Before becoming refugees, the victims may undergo experiences of pain, persecution, loss of living and family. The ultimate loss that the refugee confronts is the loss of home, and the entire context of their socio-cultural makeup. Hannah Arendt enlists their losses and laments the plight of refugees in "We Refugees":

> We lost our home, which means the familiarity of daily life. We lost our occupation, which means the confidence that we are of some use in this world. We lost our language; which means the naturalness of reactions, the simplicity of gestures, the unaffected expression of feelings (264).

They feel betrayed by the world when they leave their homeland in search of refuge. This results in a traumatic condition that is characterised by distrust and social instability. The process of the flight also turns out to be another traumatic journey that can last days or years. It is an indefinite period of ruthless situation which makes the exile vulnerable to loss and separation and become helpless witness or victim of tortures.

As stateless persons who cannot return to their homelands, their trauma remains chronic. Historical and cultural wounds reproduce themselves as they are driven out of the native soil, and wander around stateless, homeless and perpetrators continue to enjoy impunity. Thus, what refugees endure during life and leave when they are gone is a culture of pain and trauma. Though refugees are a heterogeneous group and differ tremendously in their socio-economic and professional background, resettling in the host country presents before them problems of adaptation to a new place and language under uncertain conditions and with uncertain futures. The impossibility of finding a new home necessitates establishing of a new identity as a refugee in the host country. Nevertheless, the wound inflicted on them and the trauma they suffer on being cut off from the native social matrix remains the same. It is the cultural alienation of uprootedness and homelessness that characterise the refugee experience of trauma.

Refugee trauma is one complex experience that has a communal and cultural dimension. A political, cultural, social, religious, or racial group suddenly becomes outcasts in their native country and faces persecution or is simply driven out of it to become refugees. Michael S. Roth and Charles G. Salas view collective trauma as "moments in which the normal patterns of historical continuity are strained or broken"(2) the earlier identities disintegrate. Certainly, this forced displacement has a profound traumatic impact on the individual, family and community. This interferes with the psychological and mental health, with its acculturative stress and culminates in an interminable trauma. Agonising situations encountered during the process of becoming a refugee are strong enough to cause psychological distress. Sometimes the impact can extend beyond the individual level to impinge on families and community as a whole. The trauma and its repercussions are so strong and contagious that it gets interfered with the psychosocial well-being of individuals in subsequent generations.

Though individual refugees go through unique traumatic experiences, it has a common origin. It has a communal reference and long-lasting effect. The need to be connected to their cultural heritage and the desire to preserve the native culture and identity are important factors of refugees' meaningful identity. Being uprooted from their homeland and imported to foreign soil, they constantly confront a challenged identity. The confused state between a lost past and a chaotic present can create a split not only to cultural and historical identity but also to the personal self.

Gilad Hirschberger in his essay "Collective Trauma and the Social Construction of Meaning" observes that Collective trauma is a cataclysmic experience that devastates the basic fabric of society. It creates a crisis of meaning besides the horrific loss of life. Collective trauma has an upsetting effect on individuals and groups; shatters worldviews about oneself and one's position in the world. The loss of familiar social networks is invariably hard and they often find themselves cut off from the accustomed ways of life forced to advance on a survival mode to meet the demands of a foreign environment. A depression in socioeconomic status, lower living conditions, and quasi-imprisonment organisation of refugee camps are more than enough to undo their self-esteem. Employment issues can aggravate anxiety further amidst inadequate support, and minority persecution. Such a predicament will surely make the refugees ashamed of their stigmatised identity as a besieged and 'traumatised other'. Refugees have to compromise on everything as people who had to abandon all they were familiar with. So, refugee identity is the embodiment of the traumatic experiences and their responses to these struggles.

Reinventing the lost cultural, historical legacy is the best way to reestablish the identity, and repair the traumatic past. The search for roots, meaning and identity, draws them close to the need to restore social and communal connections. It is the roots and the resulting sense of identity that posit meaning to one's existence. Collective trauma betrays the inherent sense of security with far reaching consequences upon the succeeding generations of survivors. They realise that collective memory of a calamity suffered in the past can be moulded into a vibrant strand that weaves the connection between trauma, memory and a secure identity. Thus, collective memory becomes the umbilical cord that sustains and nurtures their cultural and historic space, sense of belonging, and meaningful identity.

The effects of trauma upon identity and memory are so strong that individual and collective trauma is often discussed concerning the practice of remembering and forgetting. It is analysed as an experience anchored within the unconscious. The act of remembrance and narration inflicts psychological pain but assumes significance to an experience once subdued in the unconscious. Recollection and articulation of memories after a period of silence and suppression reorient the emotional and mental landscape of the individuals who belong to the same cultural group. The impact of the unspeakable traumatic experience upon the individual psyche gets disseminated in the collective memory of the cultural group to be circulated and transmitted along generations.

Hirschberger enlists how victims of collective trauma establish meaning from traumatic memory:

a) passing down culturally-derived teachings and traditions about threat that promote group preservation;
b) these traditions of threat amplify existential concerns and increase the motivation to embed the trauma into a symbolic system of meaning;
c) trauma fosters the sense of a collective self that is transgenerational thereby promoting a sense of meaning and mitigating existential threat;
d) the sense of an historic collective self also increases group cohesion and group identification that function to create meaning and alleviate existential concerns;
e) the profound sense of meaning that is borne out of collective trauma perpetuates the memory of the trauma and the reluctance to close the door on the past;
f) Overtime collective trauma becomes the epicenter of group identity, and the lens through which group members understand their social environment ("Collective Trauma").

The Memory of trauma its discourses try to reinstate the lost sense of community and bond with the predecessors. The impossible longing to return to the 'home' resurfaces time and again in works of literature produced by displaced communities. They resort to representations and narratives of trauma as the only possible solution to bring together the community, and preserve the traditions. That is why immigrant's loss of family, community, and external environment become themes that reverberate through creative literature. Transmitting this inheritance and voicing the pangs of rootlessness becomes a mission for those who survive the disturbing refugee reality.

This overwhelming and unnamable traumatic reality is passed on to the next generation, and they carry the memories which the first generation could not contain. Gerard Fromm in his book *Lost in*

Transmission: Studies of Trauma Across Generations proposes the idea that what human beings cannot contain and what has been traumatically over whelming, unbearable, unthinkable falls out of social discourse, but transmit into the next generation as an affective sensitivity or a chaotic urgency (xvi). Conscious or unconscious transmission of historical trauma and cultural identity prove to be an everyday reality of refugee existence. According to Eyerman, discourses on refugee trauma aims to reconfigure a group identity through shared representation, as a way of repairing the tear in the social fabric (4).

Trauma is to be resolved only when memory gets repaired. This is done through accurate representations of the suppressed voices and fears. The next generation considers it an unconscious mission to transmit the trauma by representing it as a social discourse. Addressing the heritage of trauma, the subjectivity of individual trauma is lost and becomes a discovery of the communal nature of trauma. Representation of trauma carries out the task of repairing the traumatised parent and avenging the humiliation that the community suffered. Refugees of all categories experience some kind of trauma. Because trauma is the deficiency in some of the important human needs. According to J.C. Alexander, "Human beings need security, order, love, and connection" and if something undermines these needs people feel traumatised (3). Refugees find themselves distressed, disoriented and split by the traumatic loss of security and order which they yearn for in the homeland. They bear the stamp that they do not belong to the place. That is why Liisa Malkki has suggested that refugees are a "categorical anomaly" (33) in the regular arrangement, and as such represent a political threat to the order and organisation of nations. Whereas the existing surroundings forcefully suggest that they are outsiders, identity becomes one of the major concerns for refugees who live as victims of history. This worthlessness of existence prompts them to find out their cultural roots and identity. Family interactions play a significant role in this process of meaning-making. Internally the family inculcates a spirit and memory of the homeland and hopes of return.

The traumatic event and the disruption resulting from it are preserved in a hidden form in the private sphere. Because it is pretty common that collective traumas "require a time of latency before they can be acted out, spoken about, and worked through" (Giesen 116). After the interim of suppression and silence, collective remembrance of trauma gets actively revealed in public acts of commemoration, and representations in media and literary works. As evident in the book *Baddawi,* cultural trauma finds a self-reflexive outlet for those who take upon the mission to be carriers of the original culture. Authors like Leila Abdelrazaq see this articulation as natural and necessary for reinforcing the identity and keeping the continuity of history and culture. Thus, cultural trauma discourses become instrumental in establishing and maintaining the cultural space and memory amidst humiliation and discrimination. As trauma is a destruction of meaning, resurgence from trauma requires the restoration of meaning through rebuilding hope and sense of empowerment to recoup one's being and life. However, a decontextualised analysis of trauma may marginalise the authentic local voices and cultural traditions, and thereby weaken the communities. So, the author's focus stays on the Palestinian refugee experience, its trauma and the spirit of resilience and survival that were alive in her father's life story. She makes the work echo the fragmentation of the Palestinian population, their response to trauma, social suffering etc. through meaningful collective remembrances.

Támara Hill explains that trauma can result from any circumstance that outweighs one's ability to cope, and it includes a loss of physical, emotional, psychological, or financial safety (2017). Children are more vulnerable, and prone to the trauma of relocation, resettling and the insecurity that follows. They are not at home anywhere and are badly in need of safety and security. They are destined to inherit, reflect, carry and transmit the trauma their parents experience. Tamara Hill defines inter-generational trauma as a traumatic event that began years prior to the current generation and has impacted the ways in which individuals within a family understand, cope with, and heal from trauma (2017). Children notice how parental trauma is processed, and it becomes a potential link between the experiences of traumatised refugee parents and children. Thus, parental trauma gets transformed and infused with meaning for the next generation. They find the trauma as their cultural identity and historical legacy. When identity and history are closely intertwined it culminates in a disowning of the heritage. So, every narrative of collective trauma is resistance to historical oppression, therapy for cultural wounds, and celebration of the legacy. The foremost mission of conducting this legacy is to keep associations and feel attached to the family and its inheritance and "bring its full, tragic story into social discourse" (Fromm xxi).

In such a context, narratives on refugee trauma establish an association with the heritage of the family and the community. This paper tries to place the graphic novel *Baddawi* by Leila Abdelrazaq as a work that captures and represents the trauma of dislocation and resettlement of her predecessors and transmits it to the coming generations as a legacy of historical and community trauma.

The writer dedicates the book for her grandfather and grandmother "and all the children of immigrants who have not forgotten their parent's stories" (Abdelrazaq 12). It sums up her intention to combine the experiences of different generations of Palestinians who are "born into a life of exile and persecution, indefinitely suspended in statelessness" (12). In the narration of her father's life, Leila Abdelrazaq represents the Palestinian refugee community which is the largest refugee population in the world, including the survivors of the ethnic cleansing of 1948 and their descendants.

This story is about one individual, but its anecdotes are uttered in countless families, at children's bedsides, late at night...That's because for Palestinians, preservation of the past is an act of resistance. It reminds us that we must continue to struggle, until liberation and return...This book is a testament to the fact that we have not forgotten (Abdelrazaq 12).

In the Preface the writer thus declares her solidarity with the Palestinian refugee community, however scattered they are. The motivating factor of this work is this cultural solidarity that she has inherited and wishes to hand over.

Abdelrazaq begins the narrative at the beginning of the historical trauma by exploring the life of her father in the refugee camp and goes further back to the traumatic experience of her grandparents after Nakba of 1947. The first page summarises the peaceful life of the grandparents in the family village Safsaf, as a young couple. The very next page marks the ethnic cleansing of Safsaf on 29th October 1948 when men were lined up, shot, killed, and their bodies dumped in a pit, and girls raped. "My grandparents fled Safsaf under the cover of night and walked to a refugee camp in Northern Lebanon. They thought they would be able to return home soon enough" (17). But Nakba was a catastrophe for them because Israel was established and Palestinians were barred from returning home. Hopes of return to the homeland were thwarted and thus Ahmad was born in Baddawi, a refugee camp. This sets the backdrop of Ahmad's life as a refugee in the camp. He grew up in the camp surviving on supplies for refugee children, but always exposed to news of violence and discrimination against his community.

The household was constantly a reliving of their Palestinian heritage. Mother told him stories of Palestine and exposed the kids to their festivals and staple foods. This always revived the hope that they will soon be back in their homeland. The memories and hopes of the parents got reflected in their narratives and contributed to the family dynamic. Thus, the past trauma continues to manifest itself in the present in different ways and children imbibe a collective and unconscious solidarity with the original trauma. When the Arab armies plan to fight against Israelis, it fuels their expectation to return. Mother assures Ahmad that "we can leave the camp and go back to Safsaf" (Abdelrazaq 34). "Ahmad wondered what Palestine would be like. He thought of his mother's stories. Everyone in the camp began to pack up. There was a lot of excitement" (34). However, it turned out to be a setback for the Arab armies, and more Palestinians were ethnically cleansed this second time.

"Though the family could not return to Palestine, they still held strong to their traditions." (Abdelrazaq36). The family used to visit their maternal grandparents in the nearby camp during festive seasons and "listen to stories of Palestine" (39). The camps were also under constant threat from Israeli and Lebanese armies until an agreement freed the camps from Lebanese army rule. Separation from parents and shock from the cluster bomb attacks made his Baddawi days distressing. When he joins his parents in Beirut, he missed his friends at the camp and felt the school weird. Airstrikes and reports of massacres were becoming parts of everyday reality. Frustrated, Ahmad opts to go back to Baddawi, and continue his studies. Flourishing on the love and care of family and friends, Ahmad concentrates on his studies and paves his way to becoming independent. When one of his benefactors is killed, he feels scared and insecure and sleeps with "a knife under his pillow" (100).

Ahmad frequently traveled between Beirut and Baddawi, "whichever seemed safer at the time. But really, nowhere was safe for Palestinians. In their own camps, Palestinians were slaughtered…Still, Ahmad was always trying to outrun the war" (Abdelrazaq101). His ambition to join the college made him work hard for the exam. Though he got high scores, he could not get admission as the organisation for refugees did not support him. Ahmad decides to go to America for his studies because he was sure that "Nobody in Lebanon will hire a Palestinian for a decent job" (114). With the help of his uncle in the U.S, Ahmad got admission there and worked out the formalities. Ahmad applied for his VISA. But "as a Palestinian refugee, he was a stateless person. He had no citizenship or passport, just a refugee card…Nothing was certain except that he was leaving" (115).

The narratives of collective trauma aim at establishing historical truth and healing the wounds inflicted by collective trauma. They thematically recreate the response to the social affliction, and use trauma as a political tool to echo the once silenced voice of a community and reopen the treasury of cultural memory. But the discourse of trauma is not letting everything out of the collective storehouse of memories for, such discourse, according to Wertsch, "emerges in response to the need to create a usable past" (44). It involves selective recollection and careful inclusion of events and memories to remind one only of those things from the past that one wants to remember. Cultural trauma is recognised as a disorder, but when it comes to its narrative, it shows how to remember the past in a suitable way for the benefit of the present state. Thus, memories that render comfort and grant a sense of composure are constantly recalled and compiled.

Leila Abdelrazaq, through the life story of her father, proposes to offer a wealth of material from real life and constructs a discourse to seek social agreement for interpreting the usable past and rethinking collective identity. She selects a period of acute discomfort in the life of her father, which reflects the life of every child in refugee camps, and creates a discourse out of it. Though the new generation has no direct connection with the traumatic U-turn of their predecessors, they can take part in it through collective cultural memory. The biography of Ahmad, the author's father, presents a separate and unique experience. But it remains in a particular social context, influenced by age-specific attitudes. So *Baddawi*, the biography of a Palestinian refugee, becomes the representative story of every refugee kid of that age. Cultural trauma is precisely "a collective phenomenon, a condition experienced by a group, community, or society, as a result of disruptive events culturally interpreted as traumatising" (Sztompka 458).

The book can be considered simply as a coming-of-age story presented as a graphic narrative. Nevertheless, the writer Leila Abdelrazaq, a Chicago – based Palestinian artist, in writing the biography of her father Ahmad, does not forget to represent the life and struggles of every Palestinian child raised in a refugee camp. Presenting their struggles from a child's eye view, the writer brilliantly fuses the plight of thousands of Palestinian refugees into this deeply personal story. A solemn life narrative in comic book form attracts anyone inquisitive about the predicament of Palestinian refugees.

Palestinians are the biggest refugee group and they suffer the pangs of uprooting for the longest spell in the world. Three-quarters of the Palestinian people are displaced outside the borders of their historic homeland. When the book was published in 2015, the problems of Palestinian refugees already had a history of 67 years. The current refugees are the descendants of those who had to flee from Palestine because of a policy of ethnic cleansing. Those who went through the agonising flight are thinning in number, and the present population does not have a personal memory of anything other than life in the camps. The Palestine to which they were introduced as children through stories is enormously different from the one today, for Israel had rubbed away the signs of Palestinian presence. So, it is reasonably evident that the living link the Palestinians had with their homeland is fading. In the essay "Displacement and Social Identity: Palestinian Refugees in the West Bank," George E. Bisharat observes that "Palestinians …have very strong attachments to the villages and towns of their origins, and to the land more generally" (174). Thus, despite refugee status being a stigma and mark of disgrace, the imagined past remains a moral claim and strong motivating solid for the Palestinian refugees.

Transgenerational transmission presupposes coming to know a most extensive narrative from the preceding generation. Molly S. Castelloe, in her blog 'How Trauma Is Carried Across Generations,' observes that Psychic legacies and anxieties are transferred through stories or touching emotional messages that unconsciously flow between adult and child (2012). It demands keen listening to the stories of parents and grandparents, and close observation and attention to their social and historical context and cultural tradition. To be able communicate the grief of the predecessors, the next generation has to come to grip with the trauma and find ways to represent it. Trauma being unspeakable suffering, the first-hand victims of it may not give it a right turn of phrase. However, the following generations can articulate it as they carry the parents' wound into the future. When the unspeakable traumatic past gets articulated, it exorcises the remnants of the ancestors' trauma to heal and repair the historical shame and hurt. Castelloe summarises that traumatic transmission ferries out unacknowledged grief along multiple vectors and a communal unity is subsequently created.

While transmission of trauma through literature and artistic productions heal the wounds of the preceding generation, it familiarises the following generations with the context of the original trauma and inculcates a sense of cultural pride and solidarity with the fellow beings scattered across the globe. This is where *Baddawi* the trauma narrative in the form of a comic graphic novel, becomes a significant work about Palestinian refugees. In the preface, Leila Abdelrazaq remarks: "Today, Palestinians make up the largest refugee population in the world, numbering more than five million…They live all over the world, from refugee camps across the Middle East to homes in Chicago's south suburbs. This is about one of them. He happens to be my father" (11).

The text begins at the birth of the trauma rather than at the birth of the hero. The very first statement that kicks off the story, "Palestine is buried deep in the creases of my grandmother's palms" (Abdelrazaq16) reveals how keen she is in excavating the past and its culture. The grandmother is called 'teta' by the author by the Palestinian tradition. Teta was only seventeen when her village was ethnically cleansed in 1948 Nakba. She survived the catastrophe as she could hide in a building. They started their flight thinking that it was a temporary displacement. However, after Israel was established, they barred Palestinians from returning home: "This was the Nakba, our catastrophe" (18). The writer purposefully travels back in time to discover the details about a historical event which proved to be a turning point in the destiny of all Palestinians. The narrative clarifies that whatever information she got about her homeland came from the stories remembered by her grandparents. Techniques of transmission vary; sometimes trauma is communicated by maintaining silence and sometimes by expressing hope that it would soon be over and never occur again. Distanced by two generations, Leila still cherishes the memory that's handed over by her predecessors and values it as a legacy. "Ahmad's grandparents had many traditions from Palestine. Each day, his grandfather would drink one raw egg and a small amount of olive oil. Though he was very old, he had perfect eyesight because of this daily ritual" (37). She conveys not only historical facts and geographical details but also cultural practices that characterise Palestinian life.

The technique of graphic narration is also a brilliant choice made by the writer to have an unusual approach to the traumatic incidents. Being a powerful medium to convey the complex traumatic experience, graphic novels portray the historical trauma, and unbury victims through the illustration. This iconic language makes the content easier to tackle and helps the readers to access the traumatic experience. While the content denounces the violence involved, the medium mitigates the shock and impact of traumatic experiences. Conceived as a comic for children, it facilitates intergenerational transmission of collective memory and caring for the younger generations.

Joanne Pettitt claims that "comic books and graphic novels rely on active reader responses, creating a dynamic process of interpretation that is closely linked to constructions of memory" (174). *Baddawi*, as a graphic novel, explores the experiences and memories of the actual characters under traumatising events. The artist exploits the prospects of the graphic narrative medium to depict the psychological effects of trauma on the individual subject and the group. The traumatised psyche of the victim and the community is exposed to make the readers witnesses of their distressing plight.

The artist infuses a cultural stroke to the illustrations by abundant use of the 'pixelated' looking pattern, which is connected to the traditional Palestinian embroidery. Thus, all aspects and the entire socio-cultural, political, historical scenarios of Palestinian displacement after 1948 are entrenched in the content and form of the text. The technical use of graphic language with its visual, verbal, and structural details enables the reader to view history and transform historical memory from a narrow local perspective to something of global concern.

Collective trauma can have secondary gains for the victims that must not be overlooked. The traumatising events are not always adverse in their impact. The first and direct outcome of trauma is the spirit to thrive and overcome the immediate material and emotional losses. Forced to live in survival mode, they learn appropriate methods to deal with bitter experiences and use them as potent fertilizers for personal development. As suffering can kindle a positive change in the individual, it creates a better –adapted, post-traumatic edition of the self. Harvey and Miller observe: "In the aftermath of traumatic events, most survivors are engaged in the arduous process of constructing a more positive, less threatening view of the world and themselves than that implied by the extreme experience" (36). Post-traumatic growth, one of the positive outcomes of trauma, is also manifested in the character and evolution of Ahmad. After the initial traumatisation, it instills in him a spirit of survival whereby trauma acts as a facilitator for growth. By following a redemptive storyline, the narrative finds a place for negative and positive aspects of trauma and exhibits a potential to empower self and others.

The private and the political, the solemn and the common merge into the narrative to give a comprehensive picture of the struggle and resistance of the Palestinians after their displacement. The transmission of these memories can be seen as a shared response to societal trauma. Being survivors of such disruptive experiences, their narratives, records, and expressions of cultural rituals strike the collective memory. The collective memory of the historical events thus becomes a possession of those members who were born scores of years later. This collective memory is not a precise record of history, but rather a testimony traced by group members. Still, it serves to inject meaning into traumatic history and provides a sense of the past that serves the crucial function of creating a social identity. According to Liu and Hilton, history offers us narratives which reveal who we are, where we came from and where we are heading to. Thus, it traces the path by constructing the essence of a group's identity (537).

Trauma thus serves to strengthen cultural bonds and function as building blocks of identity. Group narrative and the collective memory are rebuilt out of trauma. They get expressed in different modes of representations and enable the transmission of resilience and resistance to the succeeding generations. L.L. Braga and others recapitulate this idea by stating that "by means of poetic, epic, romanticised narratives –, turning a "cursed inheritance" of sorts into a "memorable legacy" (9).

The discourse of trauma presented in *Baddawi* begins with collective trauma. The direct victims of the catastrophe Nakba of 1948 were the writer's grandparents, when they were quite young. Ahmad, one of their sons, goes through the insecurity of the refugee camp in Lebanon. The memories of that period get transformed into a collective memory that embodies the predicament of Palestinian refugee children. The intensity of harsh experiences is subtly suggested as the focus of the discourse remains on how the protagonist adapts to the situation for his survival and outrun the trauma by leaving Lebanon in 1981. The text as a biography of Ahmad written by his daughter puts together events and memories from 1948 to 1981. Though his childhood and adolescence are traumatised and victimised, for Leila, it becomes the cue for her search for roots and identity. The trauma at the camp provides a sense of inherited history and contributes to group identification. Moving back in time, she recreates and relives the trauma of her grandparents during persecution and flight. All these memories culminate in a system of meaning and identity where she becomes a part of the transgenerational collective self.

As a trauma narrative, *Baddawi* is an attempt to open the doors to the past, and unbury the roots of identity looking through the lens of trauma. Collecting, preserving and passing down the treasured traditions remain the central aim of the book. *Baddawi* depicts how Palestinians cling to their traumatic memory as a cherished possession. Trauma thus gets represented as an agent that accelerates the process of constructing meaning around an experience of extreme adversity. It is not only the individuals who benefit from this process of meaning-making and the creation of identity. It also serves to restore a trans-generational collective self, and to patch up the historical identity. Collective trauma being an experience with real consequences for different generations, its by-product, the trans-generational collective self, also acts as a link between past, present and future members of the community.

Works Cited

Aarelaid-Tart, Aili.*Cultural Trauma and Life Stories*, Kikimora Publications, 2006.

Abdelrazaq, Leila. *Baddawi*. Just World Books, 2015.

Alexander, J.C. "Toward a Theory of Cultural Trauma". In Alexander, J. C. et al. *Cultural Trauma and Collective Identity*. U of California P, 2004.pp.1–30.

Arendt, Hannah. "We Refugees". *The Jewish Writings*, edited by Jerome Kohn et al., Schocken Books, 2007.

Batista, Elizabeth and Pinto Wiese. "Culture and Migration: Psychological Trauma in Childrenand Adolescents" *Traumatology,* vol.16, no.4, 2010, pp.142-152. doi.org/10.1177/1534765610388304.

Bisharat, George E. "Displacement and Social Identity: Palestinian Refugees in the West Bank." (Special Issue) *Population Displacement and Resettlement: Development and Conflict in the Middle East,* vol. 11, no. 4, 1994, pp.163-188. onlinelibrary.wiley.com/doi/abs/10.1111/j.2050-411X.1994.tb00806.x

Braga, L.L., et al. "Transgenerational Transmission of Trauma and Resilience: a Qualitative Study with Brazilian Offspring of Holocaust Survivors". *BMC Psychiatry*, vol.12, no.134, 2012. https://doi.org/10.1186/1471-244X-12-134

Castelloe, Molly S., "How Trauma Is Carried Across Generations": *The Me in We, Psychology Today.* 2012. www.psychologytoday.com/intl/blog/the-me-in-we/201205/how-trauma-is-carried-across-generations

Erikson, K.T. *Everything in its Path.* Simon and Schuster, 1976.

Eyerman, R. *Cultural Trauma: Slavery and the Formation of African American Identity.* CUP, 2001.

Fromm, Gerard. M (ed.) *Lost in transmission: Studies of Trauma across Generations.* Routledge, 2019. doi.org/10.4324/9780429476884.

Giesen, B. *Triumph and Trauma.* The Yale Cultural Sociology Series. Paradigm Publishers, 2004.

Harvey, J.H, Miller, E.D., editors. *Loss and Trauma: General and Close Relationship Perspective.* Routledge, 2000.

Hill, Tamara. "Should mental health professionals understand intergenerational trauma?" 18 December 2017. www.acamh.org/blog/intergenerational-trauma.

Hirschberger, G. "Collective Trauma and the Social Construction of Meaning." *Frontiers of Psychology,* vol.9, no.1441, 2018. doi.org/10.3389/fpsyg.2018.01441

Liu, J. H, and Hilton, D. J. "How the past weighs on the present: social representations of history and their role in identity politics". *British Journal of Social Psychology*, vol.44, 2006, pp.537-56.doi:10.1348/014466605X27162

Malkki, L. "Context and Consciousness: Local Conditions for the Production of Historical and National Thought among Hutu Refugees in Tanzania." *In Nationalist Ideologies and the Reduction of National Cultures*, edited by Richard Fox, American Anthropological Association, 1990, pp. 32-62.

Neil, A.G. *National Trauma and Collective Memory: Major Events in the American Century.* M. E. Shape Armonk, 2018.

O'Neill, Linda, et al. "Hidden Burdens: a Review of Intergenerational, Historical, and Complex Trauma, Implications for Indigenous Families." *Journal of Child & Adolescent Trauma*, vol.11, no.2, 2018, pp. 173–186.

doi: 10.1007/s40653-016-0117-9

Pettitt, J. "Memory and Genocide in Graphic Novels: The Holocaust as Paradigm." *Journal of Graphic Novels and Comics*, vol. 9, no.2, 2018, pp.173-186. doi:10.1080/21504857.2017.1355824.

Rapport, N. and Overing, J. *Social and Cultural Anthropology: The Key Concepts.* Routledge. 2000.

Roth, M. S. and Charles G. Salas. *Disturbing Remains: Memory, History, and Crisis in the Twentieth Century.* The Getty Research Institute. 2001.

Sangalang, Cindy C, and Cindy Vang. "Intergenerational Trauma in Refugee Families: A Systematic Review." *Journal of Immigrant and Minority Health*, vol.19, no.3, 2017, pp.745-754. doi:10.1007/s10903-016-0499-7

Sztompka, P. "Cultural Trauma: The Other Face of Social Change". *European Journal of Social Theory*, vol. 3, no. 4, 2000, pp.449–466.

CHAPTER 6

Aesthetics and Experience: Spatio-Temporal (Dis)locations in Postcolonial Trauma Cinema in India

Smitha M.

Trauma, as a social experience, was academically located and attempted analysis in the twentieth century. The many historical and socio-political events and the resultant conditions brought in newer experiences of trauma and its manifestations in everyday life. The condition of chaos and irrationality which are the essential characteristics expressed by modernity defined the twentieth century and manifested in the discourses of the age. The linearity of history could not explain the conditions. Moreover, it was broken into fragments and concepts of consciousness. These ruptures and fissures of everyday experience brought the prevalence of conditions of trauma that became characteristic of the twentieth and then later, the twenty-first century.

Trauma studies theorise an event as traumatic when it is not correctly perceived at the moment of its occurrence. This lack of realisation or perception occurs due to the surprise associated with the incompleteness of understanding of the sufferer at the moment of occurrence. This half-baked experience that is not fully realised, and resurfaces at some later point in time, appears incomprehensible in two ways. The first one being the incomprehensibility at the time of the original experience and second being that of the realisation of that inability at the later time of recollection. This complexity makes it traumatic where the space and time of the past and the present tangle up, blurring perspectives. This recurrence is called the Post Traumatic Stress Disorder (PTSD). PTSD occurs due to the incoherence of space and time of the past experience and the present reality of re-experiencing the past event or the memory resurfacing to the subject. This discordance of space and time is characteristic of trauma.

The Spatio-Temporal cartography across the past and present, remains a complicated and complex process, because both, the space and time under consideration are beyond the material space and time of everyday experience. The intrinsic fluid-like quality of the human mind also makes it a complex process. Trauma, in all its complexity, can be understood only through symbolic or abstract language. When it comes to the representation of this complexity, it is required that a medium capable of conveying the fluid nature be employed. Cinema as a medium of artistic and symbolic expression, dwells on the threshold between the expressible and the inexpressible and oscillates between the real and the imagined; the concrete and the abstract. By using various techniques, cinema is inherently capable of enabling a study of the spatio-temporal dislocation of trauma.

Cinema, by virtue of its visual characteristics and fluid medium, is capable of dwelling between the expressible and the inexpressible. This quality rightly captures the essence of trauma in its character of being unrepresentable or hardly representable. Cinema as a medium, has proven its credibility of oscillating between the real and the imagined; the abstract and the concrete. As mentioned above, trauma cinema makes use of this inherent quality of the medium to develop an aesthetic specific to the subject under consideration, that is, trauma and its representation. With the use of various cinematic techniques, including the mise-en-scene and the mise-en-shot, trauma cinema, enables a study of the spatio-temporal (dis)joints and (dis)junctures characteristic of trauma.

This paper tries to locate the dream-like, abstract nature of trauma as portrayed in the Indian trauma cinema and also attempts to decipher the aesthetics and the spatio-temporal cartography in select cinema from India that represents the trauma of the Nation-State. In an attempt to comprehend the experience of trauma in its spatio-temporal ruptures, this paper does not look into the specific theories of spatiality and temporality, but considers both as inherently fluid. This paper will focus on the theories of Susannah Radstone, Janet Walker, and Michael S Roth regarding the cinematic techniques employed by trauma cinema to capture the spatio-temporal disruptions and PTSD. While there are debates regarding the cinematic techniques best suited for the treatment and deciphering of trauma on screen, these critics are united by the concept of creating a space for active engagement by the spectator, against a passive visual consumption or a melodramatic catharsis.

Trauma Cinema emerged as one of the prominent genres of films. The abstract nature of the trauma extends beyond ordinary perceptions. The medium of cinema and its intrinsic structure enables a metaphysical perception of trauma. Trauma cinema modified its vocabulary to generate an aesthetic specific to the experience of trauma. The varied aesthetics of trauma cinema are attempts to decipher and depict trauma which is challenging to represent, preliminarily due to the difficulty in expressing faced by those who undergo trauma. This intrinsically fluid nature of the concepts of space and time, as well as the human psyche and its traumatic experiences, the method of representation and understanding requires an equally fluid medium.

As mentioned earlier, trauma is generated mainly due to the incomplete resurfacing of the prior traumatic experience because the sufferer could not comprehend the event at the moment of occurrence. Cathy Caruth, who derives her theories of trauma from Freud's concepts of non-linear experience, reformulates those theories and concentrates on the concepts of belatedness and latency of the experience.

The historical power of the trauma is not just that the experience is repeated after its forgetting, but that it is only in and through its inherent forgetting that it is first experienced at all. And it is this inherent latency of the event that paradoxically explains the peculiar, temporal structure; the belatedness, of historical experience: since the traumaticevent is not experienced as it occurs, it is fully evident only in connection with another place, and in another time (Caruth 8).

The lack of realisation of the event causes repetitions and recurrence of that event across various axes of space and time. Those recurrences manifest in fragmented forms as traumatic flashbacks, nightmares, intrusive thoughts, and repetitive re-enactments. Rather than being remembered as an event of the past, the experience of trauma becomes part of the survivor's identity and the survivor lives between the past and the present, incapable of finding the differences of space and time. This incomprehension causes a rupture in the perception of space and time by the traumatised. This blurring of space and time brings in spatial and temporal dislocations.

The experiences of spacelessness and timelessness, are due to the dislocation felt by the sufferer, which in turn, collapses the distance between the past and the present – the here and the there. The traumatised, then, is unable to differentiate between the past space and time and the present space and time. Under favourable conditions that trigger the traumatic event of the past, the memory resurfaces and evokes the past spatio-temporal experience. Furthermore, this happens as bouts of shock, anxiety, depression, thereby, disrupting the parameters of spatiality and temporality by displacements and relocations. These displacements and relocations happen in the line of space and time. Eventually, the traumatised is neither able to comprehend the space and time of the event in relation to the space and time as it occurred in the past, nor is the traumatised able to understand it in terms of space and time as it happened as the memory is recollected in the present. This leads to further confusion and lack of clarity, resulting in repression.

This psychological distress becomes the survivor's identity due to repeated repressions. "On a social, as well as, individual psychological level, the penalty for repression is repetition" (Herman 7). So, this repetition is what keeps the spatio-temporal dislocations intact and prevents the traumatised from overcoming or even understanding the rupture in spatio-temporal experience.

The ability to recover the past is thus closely and paradoxically tied up, in trauma, with the inability to have access to it. And this suggests that what returns in the flashback is not simply an overwhelming experience that has been obstructed by a later repression or amnesia, but an event that is itself constituted, in part, by its lack of integration into consciousness (Caruth 152).

Repetition and the resultant belatedness of experience of trauma prevent the traumatised from locating the experience to a single space or time. The confusion between the past and the present makes the traumatised conceive of traumatic experience as always outside the boundaries of space and time. This spatio-temporal incoherence and the timeless quality of the psyche accentuate trauma. Trauma, seen merely as an event or a condition affected upon a person, is erroneous. The socio-political framework and historical contextualisation of which trauma is a result should always be considered as the primary ground from which to approach trauma. "This isolation of a self-contained event and its trauma ignores the larger issues of systemic proportions and forces at work over a long stretch of history" (Kaplan and Wang 4).

Trauma, when seen through the postcolonial framework, generates considerations and questions of all the historical events and socio-political conditions of a collective subconscious. In the Third World countries, in a postcolonial scenario, trauma studies became an active academic field of engagement. Personal narratives of trauma could not be divorced from the violence and trauma engraved on the body of the Nation, due to the ruptures from the Colonial rule and that of nation-formation and nation-building. In the case of India, like all Nations, violence was integral to its formation and once formed into a Nation-State, it had to deal with processes of curbing down further violence to hold the national identity intact. For a better understanding of trauma, be it individual or collective, the historical and socio-political conditions of the Nation, has to be taken into consideration, as background.

From the parameters of human psychology, trauma and its nuanced experiences were attempted to be deciphered by cinema – both from the perspective of those who underwent trauma and those who tried to perceive it from an outsider's view. However, it is problematic to speak about trauma as something experienced only by those who undergo such an experience because it has permeated our world in a rhizomatic mode.

Postcolonial expression to trauma in India was an organic response to the violence embedded in the body of the nation-state. While the trauma of partition and trauma of nation-building exist as collective traumas, the archaic patterns of personal traumas added to the collectively felt trauma of postcolonial identity. Even from its nascence, cinema in India has yoked the collective and individual traumas together to weave out national narratives in the framework of the personal. This yoking of these traumas a singular has been practiced from the inception of cinema in India, mainly to please the political centres that were not very approving of this Western art. Cinema, from its early days, was a vehicle of nation-building in India.

Trauma cinema in India drew upon the traditional and folk performances and was mainly melodramatic in nature in the early phases. Cinema has been dealing with the inherent repressed violence marked upon the body of the nation-state. Trauma cinema, across the world, has developed an aesthetics of its own, with specific recurring formalistic and narrative patterns, in attempts to portray and understand the ruptures and dislocations of Space and Time. Trauma cinema differs basically concerning with the cultural expression to each country, since trauma is basically a historical and cultural phenomenon. The aesthetics aimed by the trauma cinema in India, like everywhere, demanded delivery of catharsis of a traumatic past with a historical continuum. Inscribed within the genre of melodrama is the traumatic memory of past violence and the history of Indian cinema.

The abstractness of traumatic experience is attempted to be converted into concrete terms in trauma cinema. In this process, the unthinkable is being attempted portrayal. This visual witnessing of the unthinkable is an attempt towards comprehending the spatio-temporal rupture. The complexity of the representation of trauma in cinema has resulted in creating different effects. Susannah Radstone looks at trauma cinema from the perspective of the effect it creates on the spectator. Radstone locates trauma cinema as a genre that demands active participation from the spectator. She locates the necessity of aesthetics to evoke active spectatorship. Radstone's perspective is relevant because it is the spectator and their cultural memory that trauma cinemas address.

By generating a visual representation of an experience that could not be communicated plainly in words, trauma cinema presents the spectator with an experience of experiencing the unthinkable. The spectator could or could not be a first-hand victim of the specific traumatic situation portrayed in the cinema. Such a situation is applicable, both to collective traumas like partition or terrorist attacks and to individual traumas like rape or domestic violence. In trauma cinema, the discourse could be seen, "less as defined by content than by the attempt to discover a form for presenting that context which mimics some aspects of post-traumatic consciousness itself – to reproduce for the spectator an experience of once again seeing the unthinkable" (Kaplan & Wang 19).

Trauma cinema, in order to enable visualisation of incredible traumatic experience and the post-traumatic conditions generate a visual language to enable catharsis and ownership of the traumatic memory. The aesthetics of trauma cinema contains trauma-ridden narrative induced with shock to enable historical understanding and positioning. Trauma cinema is characterised by the prominence of the cinematic language and the treatment of the national identity and thereby, eliciting traumatic pasts as narratives to be comprehended. In order to locate and understand the traumatic event – collective or individual, trauma cinema employs its techniques of spatio-temporal cartography through the self of the trauma inflicted character(s). This visual witnessing of the unthinkable is an attempt towards understanding the spatio-temporal dislocations caused by the traumatic experience during the event and the PTSD. The re-creation of the traumatic events on the screen involves spectacular and violent representations.

The endless reproduction and dissemination of trauma are achieved in trauma cinema by using documentaries, photos, newspaper cuttings and newsreels in the fictional narrative. These insertions enable the recollection of the latent memory of a traumatic event in the Nation's history. The use of voice-over as a technique to hint at an omniscient narrator, helps to naturalise the whole event. Moreover, it gives a detachment needed in trauma cinema. Trauma cinema provides a deliberate shock to the viewers by employing a detached camera at a traumatic sight and by stripping off the emotional connection from the eyes of the person involved. Scenes of violence in the partition films are replete with such technical instances where scenes of violence – both individual and collective, are shown from a detached perspective.

Even while the narration is from a personal point of view, regarding an event of collective trauma, the detached camera is employed alongside dramatic sounds of traumatic suffering and techniques like image overlap and swift editing are employed. The testimony scene in Mani Ratnam's *Dil Se*, where Meghna (played by Manisha Koirala) narrates the traumatic experiences of violence upon her family, the whole experience, is telescoped into that experience of a community, in general. The camera, from an objective perspective, records the traumatic events and the PTSD of Meghana by overlapping her image with that of the traumatic past. In this scene, the past and present space and time, overlap and the spectator experience the traumatic dishevel of space and time. "… flashbacks as evoking are presentation of trauma, as one of the more piercing depictions of memory flashes to be found anywhere in film. The staccato crosscutting of past and present builds a visual power through images that graphically match yet both compare and contrast symbolically" (Turim 209). Trauma cinema aims at generating the specific aesthetics and to understand the spatio-temporal dislocations by the use of cinematic techniques in two different ways through the mise-en-scene and mise-en-shot. Trauma films, in contradistinction to the classical regime, "dismember" by drawing on innovative strategies for representing reality obliquely, by looking to mental processes for inspiration, and by incorporating self-reflexive devices to call attention to the friability of the scaffolding for audiovisual historiography (Walker 19).

Essentially, in cinema studies, mise-en-scene and mise-en-shot are located against each other in terms of representational purpose and generation of aesthetics. One way of representing the spatio-temporal dislocations is by accentuating the speed and tempo of the narrative by bringing in rapid cuts, swift camera movements, montage and sudden bursts of sounds. Another set of techniques employed in trauma cinema renders a different language altogether, which contrasts with the first one, that is, the use of long shots, a static camera and excessive long takes. Some films present a combination of these two techniques as well. The second school mostly belongs to the art-house category of trauma cinema. Trauma cinema, in either of the above cases, brings in the same sort of deviation upon space and time that trauma causes. Trauma cinema, in its attempts to understand trauma through spatio-temporal dislocations and ruptures, employs techniques to stretch and collapse the vectors of space and time in the narrative. The above-mentioned school of trauma cinema achieves the stretching and collapse by reducing the duration of representing space and time on the screen. Such trauma cinema presents experiences that cannot be expressed in realistic terms, and enables portrayal through what Janet Walker calls, the "quality of exaggeration" (213). This school of trauma cinema compresses space-time, while the second one stretches the dimensions of space and time for the spectator. This is employed to dwell upon the traumatic space-time experience. The two methods are used in opposition to each other because of the specific aesthetics to render the traumatic experience on screen. The first method widely employs the rapid editing technique called montage, while the second technique employed by slow cinema uses long takes.

Montage is an editing technique that employs fast-paced intercutting of shots assembled from different spatial and temporal points. Long takes are shots that mostly use a stationary camera to intrigue a particular space for a prolonged period. "But from the perspective of the material turn to history, the two methods seemed to be touching base. In response to the historical crisis, both techniques effected an intensified, engaged relation to external reality" (Wang 234). While the montage creates a sort of panic in the spectator, long takes also are successfully communicate trauma by prolonged engagement of the spectator with the traumatic event. Both techniques generate an aesthetic experience of trauma that deconstructs spatio-temporal imaginings and represents the spatio-temporal rupture that is characteristic of trauma. Spatio-temporal ruptures and dislocations on-screen enable the spectator to achieve an experience otherwise too fluid to be represented. Both montage and long takes generate more meaning than on the surface. Montage achieves this "... by splicing common sense reality, by yoking/cutting discrete, monadic, heterogeneous objects violently together" (Wang 86). The technical aspects of montage, described by Eisenstein, replicate the spatio-temporal ruptures experienced by the traumatised.

Montage is employed in trauma cinema to achieve an active spectator base. It does not allow a passive visual consumption but enables an active involvement of the spectator, as Radstone says should be the objective of trauma cinema. In trauma cinema, then, montage acts"... as a crucible of trauma, rupture, and becoming; as an experiment with conflicting options and ideological positions. It touches history at a moment when it is shaken with shocks" (Wang 236). As a cinematic technique it has historically been associated with radical cinema, carrying in itself the political trauma of authoritarianism. Other cinematic effects conjoined with montage are the techniques of non-linearity, fragmentation, non-synchronous sounds, repetition, rapid editing and uncommon camera angles. Janet Walker says that it gives a "quality of exaggeration" to the traumatic events represented in the movie (Walker, 213). Such exaggerations are attempts to represent the abstractness of the experience. Such techniques try to address the traumatic history of the Nation. It also gives shape to an abstract experience. The aesthetics of tension generated by such swift and rapid movement of images on screen communicates the modernist experiences of being fragmented. Mary Ann Doane states that frames of such rapid tension are "potentially traumatic for the spectator" (15).

Maureen Turim, uses the term "traumatic flashback films" to denote to such trauma cinema. Turim adds that such films are "abrupt, fragmentary and repetitive by nature" (207). Doane's and Turim's description of trauma cinema based on the cinematic techniques employed talks about the aesthetic experience specific to trauma cinema in generating spatio-temporal ruptures and dislocations. "…fragmented editing and the use of extreme camera angles create in viewers a sense of disorientation and moral ambiguity designed to echo the experience of combat trauma" (Walker 20). The interchanging and mixing up of scattered, frozen and rapid segments of spatial and temporal dimensions in the trauma cinema that employ a fast diegetic mechanism in which montage is a prominent element is a modernist technique. While such trauma cinema can capture the traumatic experience through speedy aesthetics, some critics oppose the method. The problems of such cinema are raised as, "the truth-as-correspondence promised by realism is undercut by modernist innovations. These innovations often call attention to the processes of representation so as to emphasise that we never have unmediated access to the occurrence to which we are trying to refer" (Roth 94).

Critics like Michael S. Roth believe that the overdose of such techniques eclipses the trauma because the spectacle holds the spectator's attention. Roth opines that the shocking camera of these fast-paced techniques generates the aesthetics of further shock and alienation, which prevents the spectator from addressing the traumatic event or condition connected to the national history. Roth believes in the second category of trauma cinema that facilitates a physical encounter of the space and time of trauma to the spectator. While montage makes the spectator drift through fragments of traumatic space and time, slow cinema by employing extreme long takes, immerse the viewer in the trauma. Moreover, because this engagement happens from an outside perspective, it generates an aesthetic of catharsis, wherein PTSD is felt through the screen space and time.

Cinematic slowness in the second category of trauma cinema emerges as an alternative approach to an on-screen representation of trauma. While trauma cinemas engaging montage and other fast-paced cinematic techniques deal with both the event of trauma and PTSD, slow trauma cinema engages in the understanding of the traumatic event through the comprehension of the post-traumatic self. The slow trauma cinema deals with the duration of trauma and not on instantaneity. Slow trauma cinema challenges the standard aesthetic techniques in order to consider trauma as a condition against the perspective of trauma as an event. Even while considering trauma as a condition, slow trauma cinema tries to decipher it in terms of space and time.

Third cinema in India has extensively depended upon slow trauma cinema to drive at the condition of traumatic existence in a postcolonial, newly formed nation-state. Slow trauma cinema has its aesthetics in strict contrast to that of commercial cinema. Despite the inherent difference in aesthetics and techniques specifically used, both these categories of movies use specific techniques to locate the individual from the midst of a collective traumatic event. The use of wide-angle shots to locate the individual in a large scene is a popularly used technique to locate the subject in relation to the environment and the diegesis.

To portray collective trauma, especially of the national cause, the traumatic potential of the event is enabled by positioning the event or the character pertaining to the situation. The mise-en-scene gains importance here. In such trauma films the human condition is shown by employing the techniques of close-ups and long shots, in contrast to each other. The close-ups show individual bodies in conditions unsuited for a civilised existence. The long shots are also employed to generate the same aesthetics of sympathy and empathy. Long shots are used to place the individual in the context, where mass of human bodies lay piled or dumped on the earth. Partition movies like *Pinjar, Tamas, Hey Ram* are replete with such shots. These movies also use actual footage to highlight the experience of the event in a dehumanised form. These techniques generate an aesthetic of shock and recollection of the past traumatic events from the national memory. The aesthetics of these movies aim at recreating the eye-witness. These movies form a historical continuum and are recalled into the spectator's consciousness during later cinematic experiences.

Slow trauma by using long takes and wide-angle shots focus on trauma's latency period and how it affects the spatio-temporal perceptions of traumatised. Slow trauma cinema is also characterised by flashbacks and over stimulation of sensory feelings through the stretching of space and time from the realistic impressions. Lutz Koepnick proposes that slowness can provide "intriguing perspectives" in understanding the condition (191). The slow development of the traumatic symptoms in trauma's latency and belatedness is the specific experience that slow trauma cinema tries to develop through the aesthetics of slowness.

The loose episodic narratives, concentration on mundane activities and details, especially in domestic spaces are placed in the cinematic frame and stretched beyond the real spatio-temporal axis to generate the aesthetics of ruptures and dislocations in space and time in slow trauma cinema. In such cinema, the duration of post-traumatic memory is portrayed by the dwelling of the traumatised in domestic spaces, which once held a kind of normalcy that a pre-traumatic condition would provide. The slow trauma cinema, like the Italian neo-realists employ non-professional actors. Such a process helps in a detached perspective of the traumatic duration, unhinged by previous spectatorial expectations or memories.

The slow trauma cinema, while engaging in temporal elasticity to address temporal collapse tries to provide a physical encounter with the space in the context of PTSD and is a method of drawing a connection of the space to the psyche. The domestic space becomes radically defamiliarised and the extreme long shots screen repetitive engagements with the space to comprehend the belatedness of traumatic experience (Vidler 1992). The stretching of time and preoccupation of limited space creates a sensation of multiple spaces at the same time and it is this sensation that the long shots try to frame in slow trauma cinema. The temporality is also felt in non-linear terms because of the prolonged engagement of the traumatised with the spatial configurations.

Repetition of experiencing and expressing trauma is the primary concern of slow cinema while employing the aesthetics of temporal stagnancy. Lutz Koepnick perceives slowness in cinema as "a powerful means to remember and rework traumatic residues and reanimate painful histories seemingly frozen in the past" (Koepnick 46).The quality of cinema as a visual medium to re-enact and reproduce trauma is best explored in trauma cinema. Furthermore, no other artistic or symbolic medium is capable of dealing with the complex theme of skewed spatio-temporal structure through a seemingly commonplace experience of visual testimony.

The facilitation of witnessing of collective as well as individual trauma, provided by both the fast and slow trauma cinema, helps the spectator in negotiating the traumatic history and historical continuum of the nation-state. Trauma cinema, through varied techniques generates an aesthetics that helps the spectator understand the traumatic cultural symptoms of everyday life. India, with its colonial past, blood-stained history of nation-formation and "in the national allegory of Third World cinemas, on the other hand, the individual story typically aspires to merge into a unity with the social, so that it becomes a part of communal or national destiny" (Wang 232). In films like *Mumbai Meri Jaan* and *A Wednesday*, the individual trauma caused due to a collective tragedy act in a symbiotic nature. Each spring from the other and manifests the other.

Politically trauma cinema carries the traumatic motif ahead to serve political purposes. Trauma cinema, instead of attempting erasure of the trauma, carries its traces forward in order to maintain a national memory and thus, an identity. Trauma cinema in India has to be seen in the background of imperialism, colonialism, residual feudalism, and traumatic social conditions faced by every Third World Country. Trauma cinema, by framing spatio-temporal ruptures, attempts to shock a consumption society into facing the calamities and problems natural to the Indian context.

> The trembling of places of trauma, felt as the experience of unreality becoming real ... is proof of the close relationship between materiality and spectrality. The spectre becomes visible as the scene establishes a portal between the past and the present. The result of this opening is the sense of the ruin – in both its natural and built environment – becoming possessed by a past that cannot be reconstructed in a conventional narrative. The ruins of trauma do not redeem time and experience from annihilation and rupture, but help us to understand the structure of 'unclaimed experience' by mirroring our own attempt at giving presence to a place that refuses all evidence of presence (Trigg 99-100).

Every Nation, in its process of building up individual identities, recollects and reformulates its cultural memories. The traumatic past is recollected and re-enacted ritually through trauma cinema both for those who underwent it and those who imagine it. The ritual re-enactment occurs by engaging in a cartography of the space and time in all its ruptures and dislocations. The aesthetics of the trauma cinema aims at an emotional catharsis to assert and hold on to the construction of the nation-state. The unique character of all Third World cinema is to project the individual trauma into a collective trauma, which helps in cementing the collective force of the national identity. The spatio-temporal ruptures and dislocations in the imaginings of the national self are thus, attempted analysis through the aesthetics of national identity, by cross-cutting and prolonged brooding on the event and condition of trauma.

Works Cited

Caruth Cathy. *Trauma: Explorations in Memory.* The Johns Hopkins UP, 1995.

Doane, Mary Ann. The Emergence of Cinematic Time: Modernity, Contingency, the Archive. Harvard UP, 2002.

Herman, Judith Lewis. Trauma and Recovery: From Domestic Abuse to Political Terror. Harper Collins, 1992.

Kaplan, E. Ann and Ban, Wang, editors. *Trauma and Cinema: Cross-Cultural Explorations.* Hong Kong U. P, 2004.

Koepnick, Lutz. *On Slowness-Toward an Aesthetic of the Contemporary.* Columbia University Press, 2014.

Radstone, Susannah. "Trauma Theory: Contexts, Politics, Ethics", *Paragraph,* vol. 30, no. 1, 2007, pp. 9-29.

Ratnam, Mani. Director. *Dil Se.* 1998

Roth, Michael S. *Memory, Trauma, and History: Essays on Living with the Past.* Columbia UP, 2012.

Trigg, Dylan. "The place of trauma: Memory, hauntings, and the temporality of ruins." *Memory Studies,* vol. 2, no. 1, 2009, pp. 87-101.

Turim Maureen. "The Trauma of History: Flashbacks upon Flashbacks". *Screen,* vol. 42 no. 2, 2001, pp. 205-210.

Vidler, Anthony. *The Architectural Uncanny: Essays in the Modern Unhomely.* The MIT P, 1992.

Walker, Janet. *Trauma Cinema: Documenting Incest and the Holocaust.* U of California P, 2005

Wang, Ban. "Illuminations from the Past: Trauma, Memory, and History in Modern China." *The China Journal,* vol. 53, 2005, pp.189-190.

CHAPTER 7

Witnessing Trauma Inscribed upon Bodies: The Dichotomy of Experiences in Franz Kafka's *In the Penal Colony*

Smrithi M. Venugopal

Stretching back to at least Aristotle, 'trauma' resultant of torture has played an essential part in medieval European jurisdiction. Torture, ordered by the magistrate, was part of the law of evidence and also a legal procedure. Within the ambit of law, torture was also used as a means of punishment and ensuring justice. With the emergence of enlightenment and the movement towards humanism, torture was substituted by the modern evidentiary system. However, torture continues to be a form of coercion, confession, and control in modern societies. Torture has been used by colonial regimes to control native populations, while despots continue to use it as a means of checking dissent. Discourses and investigations on trauma and torture tend to dismiss the general assumption that accuses a single man or a small group of instigating and carrying out acts of brutality, as history exposes how military and government were also involved in perpetrating violence and torture.

Having witnessed the series of executions in London, followed by the restoration of the monarchy in 1660, Samuel Pepys, on 13th October, 1660, famously documented in his diary, an eyewitness account of the execution of a victim:

> "I went out to Charing Cross to see Major-General Harrison hanged, drawn, and quartered, which was done there. He was looking as cheerful as any man could do in that condition. He was presently cut down, and his head and heart shown to the people, at which there was great shouts of joy" (*Diary Entries*).

Witnessing executions have never gone out of fashion. Be it beheading, stoning, crucifixion, or hanging, throughout history, all gruesome and blood-chilling execution methods ever invented have proved that humankind has mastered the art of torture and death, mutilation and deformation. History has shown us how surprisingly and disturbingly 'creative' humans are in the act of inflicting pain. Silvia Amati Sans points out: "Torture is an organised instrument of social and political power, the principal aim of which is to provoke catastrophic fear and traumatic consequences throughout an entire population" (3). Whether with the use of scorching heat, sharp tools, or ravenous animals, the ingenuity that has gone into the act of torture is genuinely shocking. Execution methods that ensure slow and agonising torture, where the condemned does not immediately fall unconscious out of shock, or fall dead in a couple of minutes, are the most dreadful. In execution methods like impalement in which victims were skewered through their midsection; 'blood eagle' where the ribs of the victim were exposed and forcibly bent; others like keelhauling in which the victim is dragged through the water under the keel of a ship, flaying or skinning the victim alive; scaphism where a victim is tied in between boats or in a hollowed tree trunk and force-fed milk and honey attracting insects and files and left to die slowly and painfully in his vomit and excreta; or quartering in which a victim's body is torn apart by tying his hands and legs to horses moving in different directions, death would generally come as a result of blood loss and unbearable shock. However, the victim could be kept in a state of perpetual agony for several hours or days until they finally succumb to their severely infected wounds. Exposed, bleeding, and writhing in agony, the victim is a spectacle. Despite the gruesome nature of such executions, these were often public and attended by large, jeering crowds. Most execution methods of the past were devised in such a manner that the process of execution went on for a long time, so as to keep the tortured alive, to intensify his trauma, and to guarantee the spectators of trauma, a feeling of contentment and gratification.

Before the French Revolution, various methods were employed in putting a prisoner to death – regicides were quartered, thieves hanged, and highwaymen broken on the wheel. Only the privileged were despatched swiftly, if they were lucky, by beheading. The revolution extended this privilege to all social classes and ushered in an age when public execution was a swift and mechanised business. It was performed efficiently and on an industrial scale during the Reign of Terror by the guillotine. Holocaust reinforced the idea that torture was not a thing of the past. Survivors of medical experiments conducted in concentration camps by notorious physicians like Josef Mengele at Auschwitz such as amputations and surgeries, pressure chambers, drug tests, eye color conversion, chemical injection etc, are still not out of the terror and trauma holocaust offered (Blakemore).

In *In the Penal Colony* (1919), composed many years before the Second World War, Kafka seems prophetic of the extermination and genocide methods later developed by the Nazis in concentration camps. Kafka portrays the execution of a condemned man by a horrific killing machine. As the story goes forward, we learn that the prisoner being executed has had no trial, nor is he aware of the charges against him, and also that he is unaware of his death sentence about to be inscribed on his flesh. As the Officer carrying out the execution observes, the victim did not have to know the nature of his crime as he would very soon learn it through his bodily pain. The machine holds several needles that penetrate deep into the victim's flesh, thereby spelling out the charges in the unreadable text on the condemned man's skin. The script becomes increasingly evident over the twelve excruciating hours the victim is subjected to the killing device.

Kafka's execution machinery functions at the expense of human rights. It raises several questions about humanity and the cultural understanding of torture and trauma. Kafka enables his readers to empathise through their senses and experiences and thereby learn through their bodies. Readers might imagine themselves as the condemned one, the nameless and the faceless victims who know not their crime. Several such faceless victims and the trauma of the torture they survived or failed to survive still haunt human history.

Literature and Trauma

Pain, torture, and trauma are literary subjects that humanity has always been interested in, driven by life-death instinct, which Freud refers to as eros and thanatos respectively. The representation of torture in political speeches, in news media and books, television and film, has placed it at the forefront of our current cultural awareness. In the field of trauma studies, Sigmund Freud's detailed approaches were the earliest. They were published in his highly influential work, *Beyond the Pleasure Principle* (1920). References to trauma and its effects can be seen in his other works, like *Moses and Monotheism*, and *The Aetiology of Hysteria.* Freud first gave a detailed account about traumatic neurosis in *Beyond the Pleasure Principle.* Hence the origin of trauma theory can be attributed to psychological sources but is more empathetically and powerfully articulated in literary theory, criticism, and practice.

It was with the publication of Cathy Caruth's *Unclaimed Experience: Trauma, Narrative, and History* (1996), that the field of trauma studies in literary criticism gained significant attention. Caruth describes trauma as "an overwhelming experience of sudden or catastrophic events in which the response to the event occurs in the often delayed, uncontrolled repetitive appearance of hallucinations and other intrusive phenomenon" (32). Caruth explores how the texts of psychoanalysis, literature, and literary theory all speak about and speak through the profound story of traumatic experience. Trauma theory, in its initial course, popularised the idea of trauma as an event that has been experienced but cannot be represented again. Physical trauma that enters the psyche is so anomalous or overwhelming that it cannot be processed or comprehended by conscious memory, yet is still present in mind like an intruder or a ghost (Balaev1-14). Shoshana Felman's engagement with trauma began with her essential book (written in collaboration with psychoanalyst Dori Laub) *Testimony: Crises of Witnessing in Literature, Psychoanalysis, and History* (1992). In the 2002 book *The Juridical Unconscious: Trials and Traumas in the Twentieth Century*, Felman explores the relationship between literature and psychoanalysis to trauma and testimony and critical studies. Caruth and Felman, both insist on understanding of traumatic events and listening to the indirect expressive experiences. Freud and Breuer, in their studies on hysteria, characterised the memory of trauma as "a foreign body which long after its entry must continue to be regarded as an agent that is still at work" (Breuer 6). The late 20th century, however, brought with it the rise of trauma studies, and studying the psychological nature of trauma allows us to show how characters are affected by their traumatic histories and how their ability or inability to cope with trauma drives the action of their stories. When a character is "diagnosed" as a trauma victim, his journey can be understood through what science knows about trauma and the post-traumatic process, allowing us to explore the relationship between literature and trauma.

Earlier scholarship shaped the theory of trauma by popularising the idea of an unrepresentable event. According to Michael Richardson, scholars such as Cathy Caruth and Shoshana Felman brought psychoanalysis and post-structural deconstruction together to argue that representation of trauma depend on the paradox of speaking of what cannot be spoken. Richardson, in his *Gestures of Testimony: Torture, Trauma and Affect in Literature*, considers trauma to be "inseparable from the tension between the event and its haunting return" (104). According to him, trauma fails to belong to memory and tortures the psyche every time it revisits the mind, wounding it anew in every return. Richardson's task was to illuminate how literature might do this crucial work of recording traumatic experiences brought about by torture. He begins his discourse with an extended reflection on the very nature of torture and analysis how torture imprints on the bodies of victims and the psyche of perpetrators and witnesses alike. Early in his book, Richardson notes a curious gap. Contemporary literature, he observes, has had very little to say on the subject of torture in modern times (Richardson 6–7). Despite profusions of novels about 9/11 attacks and films that engage torture directly, Richardson observes, "this particular literary muteness persists, impoverishing our collective understandings – political, ethical, and most especially, affective – of torture" (114). In the subsequent chapters, Richardson raises questions on the various actions by which trauma and torture are documented. He identifies reading, seeing, writing, and witnessing as the tools of recording trauma. Torture thus becomes relatable and identifiable to the readers.

> Torture should be known, not simply in the abstract – as something that happens over there, to someone else – but as an experienced event, one with a terrible and traumatic aftermath (Richardson 9).

In his second chapter on reading torture, Richardson discusses the difficulties of writing about an experience that is painful and damaging, both physically and psychologically. Richardson's materiality of language, in the choice of pain-signifiers like 'burning, searing, stinging … cutting, piercing, crushing' (Richardson 49) is also notable. Richardson also calls upon Kafka and Coetzee in his discussion of the moral dilemmas and political ambiguities of bearing the responsibility of writing on torture and subsequent trauma. Richardson spends the remainder of the book exploring ways that authors might write what many can scarcely imagine.

Richardson probes into the cultural, political, and aesthetic elements of torture and creates a four-dimensional mesh of the perpetration, perpetuation, politicisation, and representation of trauma and torture.

As Rebecca Adelmann points out in her review of Richardson, torture was supposedly an interrogative technique, and much of its literary incidence was punitive. The texts were implicitly and sometimes explicitly, creating distinctions between the different ways in which torture could be utilised to foster a more critical and even constructive kind of ambivalence. According to Adelmann, Richardson constructs an expansive archive, "the inventiveness of which lies not so much in content but arrangement." Richardson reads familiar artifacts like Franz Kafka's In the Penal Colony as prescient of contemporary tortures and as genealogical markers that contain hints about how those tortures might someday be written (Adelmann 719-20).

Medieval scholars tend to be frustrated by the excess of torture and brutality in the society back during the middle-ages, as the modern visions of the medieval societies construct the former as endemically violent, and cruel. Although medievalists themselves have produced a significant body of research to refute the historical generalisation that the middle-ages were necessarily inhuman, there is certainly room for more. However, the modern society also cannot be considered humane either, even though it is supposedly driven by humanistic values.

Larrisa Tracy, in her path-breaking work *Torture and Brutality in Medieval Literature*, attempts a revisionist approach that exculpates the middle-ages of the stigma of torture. Medieval and early modern literary depictions of torture and brutality, argues Tracy, was "not mimetic" but served the purpose of dissent, satire, and critique (1-2). Tracy observes that analysis of torture as a cultural signifier and a mode of dissent is absent in literature (17). In her final chapter, Tracy acquaints her readers with the early modern English world and argues that the early modern writers and playwrights attempted "to situate excessive brutality outside the realm of their consciousness as something archaic or 'medieval'" (291).

Hanna Skoda, in her review of Tracy's text, observes how Tracy's wide-ranging work exposes and examines the "notorious prevalence of torture and physical violence in medieval literature" and discusses how the text offers compelling insights into the function of torture as a rhetorical device (121). In her opinion, Tracy has done a fine job of reading through an impressive range of texts to expose the didactic and discursive functions of torture in medieval literature. Tracy has analysed in detail the different motifs of torture and brutality in a wide range of medieval literary texts. Tracy argued that the many instances of violence should not be read as reflective of the "reality" of medieval life, but instead should be understood as negotiating cultural anxieties about emerging national identities. The comparative dimension in Tracy, as Skoda observes, in the use of torture as a literary device is highly compelling as she ranges her work from English hagiography to Icelandic sagas attending to their exciting commonalities. Tracy shows how practices of torture were on the rise in England, by the early modern period, and representation of torture in the literature of the period aimed not to mimic, but to critique and to problematise that surge in a variety of ways. Skoda observes, "one way was to demonise the medieval period as an era of excessive brutality," a discourse which is in many ways responsible for our modern popular stereotypes of the cruel Middle Age (122). As Welsh points out, Tracy's instances of torture and brutality in the texts that she chose, served didactic purposes that taught the reader of the ambiguities and anxieties of national identities rather than serve the mimetic purpose of reflecting societal realities in the medieval period (604).

Elaine Scarry, in *The Body in Pain: The Making and Unmaking of the World*, discusses the rarity with which physical pain is represented in literature as "most striking when seen within the framing fact of how consistently art confers visibility on other forms of distress" (19). Psychological suffering, however, seems to have a referential content even though it is difficult to express, and varies from one person to another. Scarry wrote, "physical pain is language destroying" (19). Physical pain does not only resist language, but also actively destroys it. Scary analyses physical suffering and its relation to the multiple vocabularies and cultural forces that confront it, like the literary, political, philosophical, medical, and religious.

Trauma as Spectacle

Execution was once a public spectacle. In Britain, public hangings were for a long time a massive source of popular entertainment. Large crowds of men and women, including children, would travel long distances to be part of the occasion. An Act of Parliament ended public hangings in Britain in 1868, but it took America nearly seventy more years to follow suit. The United States had public executions of the condemned criminals well into the twentieth century. In 1936, Rainey Bethea, an Afro-American who confessed to rape and murder of an older woman was the last to be publicly executed in America. Considering his execution, in *The Last Public Execution in America*, Perry T. Ryan reports that "the Rainey Bethea trial is one of the most celebrated trials in Kentucky history. Thousands of people attended the hanging, which left a lasting impression in the minds of all who witnessed it" and around "20,000 men, women and children witnessed it" (1). Reports of the crowd surging forward to grab 'souvenirs' from the dead man appear to be exaggerated, although they were instrumental in the abolishing of public execution in the United States.

Public executions, in civilised societies, began to be looked upon as a matter of embarrassment as our society was shamed into drawing a line between public executions and entertainment. Most civilised societies of today look upon public executions with distaste. Earlier, in the minds of those watching, public execution was an affirmation that justice was being delivered. Kafka's plot introduces a character visiting a penal colony, expected to attend an execution of a soldier alleged to have disobeyed his superior, and state a verdict regarding the nature of punishment, and delivery of justice. The traveler turns into the witness to the spectacle of execution, one among the many who have watched similar things happening in the past.

The key focal point of the story is an ancient machine programmed to inflict torture and bodily destruction. Not just the victim, but also the tool, is a spectacle. It is a matter of awe and admiration. Kafka's killing machine is perhaps one of the most horrific killing apparatuses ever conceived in history and literature. For Heinz Politzer, for instance, the essence of *In the Penal Colony* is the execution machine, which becomes for him a symbol for "the tortures to which Kafka, the writer, subjected himself" (104). The Officer at the Penal Colony is obsessed with the artistry of the elaborate apparatus and expresses his respect to the old Commandant who created it. The entire first half of the story involves the Officer's enthusiastic description of the structural peculiarities of the machine. Such attention has been given to accomplish the machinist functions of the apparatus and to the discourses on the same. The description of the artistic design of the brutal machine occupies a significant portion of the text. The bed, numerous needles, a harrow, straps for hands and feet, the disgusting and bloodied mouth felt, the inscriber and the batteries, a spout that squirts water to wash the blood of the inscription and keep it clean and clear, and the electrically heated bowl of rice soup beneath the head, show the gruesome nature of the notorious machine.

The ethical issues generated by the hurtful machine are not addressed by the officers. The architect of the machine was keen on thinking about how his creation will affect the bodies it subjugates. From numerous tiny needles that slowly inscribe the text, to the final stab that eventually kills the victim; the machine is perfected for torture. The story is highly corporal in how power operates, and architectures and institutions of power capture bodies and torture them. When the Officer despairs convincing the traveler of the efficacy of the machine, he puts an end to the torment of the condemned and frees him. Instead, the officer offers himself to the machine. The machine breaks down bloodily, executing the Officer. Kafka depicts the devastating effects of bodily subjection when the machine itself disintegrates. The victims of trauma in the Penal Colony are unable to process their trauma. Nor do they remain alive to relate to others the traumatic experiences they have endured. The gruesome brutalities in the Officer's tale of spectator punishment tell of a world in which "the very excess of the violence employed is one of the elements of its glory"; the apparatus demonstrates a "justice [that] pursues the body beyond all possible pain" (Foucault 34).

Witnessing Public Executions

From ancient to contemporary times, it is the witness who makes the process of the production of torture meaningful. The trauma of the victims becomes complete only when the witnesses of trauma abet its production, and play a complicit part in the process. According to Ballengee, it is the presence of the witness that gives a rhetorical aspect to the practice of torture. She argues that the audience, or the witness, is the critical element in the "successful" practice of torture in its political province. The rhetorical function further heightens through a combination of visual spectacle, narration, and performance. In her opinion, every literary text, in its representation of torture before a witnessing audience, emphasises the visual spectacle, relies on linguistic and imagistic tools, and situates the discourses of torture in a civic context (3).

In his precaution against subordinating others, Friedrich Nietzsche warns that "we shall seldom be able to alter an individual and, if we should succeed in doing so, something else may also succeed perhaps unawares: we may have been altered by him" (140). In penal societies, like the one envisaged by Kafka, witnessing executions is also about bearing witness to what the government was doing to its citizens. It is difficult to arrive at a definite answer as to why some people watched gruesome executions with fascinations, why some others were revolted by the sight of another person in pain, while some others seemed indifferent to the whole process. Executions served as group bonding exercise that reinforced social norms, and revived the thrill of the spectacle, while governments intentionally ritualised the process to demonstrate political control. The affair of execution had a carnival feel. The spectators sang and chanted while street vendors sold eatables. Kafka presents to the reader, relics of the same carnival spirit; a crowd waiting to witness a gory killing, along with cheering women and children, who are offered the privilege of special seats to experience an uninterrupted panoramic view of the site of execution, the victim and the process of torture. It is no wonder that the children, who are conditioned from their early childhood to witness executions and thereby form primary notions upon the exercise of power and delivery of justice, to be indifferent to the trauma of the victim in their adulthood. The execution Officer considers himself to be the only defender of the old way, and advocate and open supporter to the legacy of the old Commandant. His memories of the most spectacular executions carried out by the "peculiar apparatus", when no discordant notes disturbed the killing machine, is worth mentioning. Being the only person to witness all the executions carried out by the machine, and eventually becoming the final victim of the disintegrating apparatus, the Officer's memories carry the weight of nostalgia as he expresses his pain in performing executions with a partially damaged machine with no public to witness.

> You should have seen the executions in earlier days! The entire valley was overflowing with people, even a day before the execution. They all came merely to watch. Early in the morning, the Commandant appeared with his women. Fanfares woke up the entire campsite. I deliver the news that everything was ready. The whole society – and every high official had to attend – arranged itself around the machine. This pile of cane chairs is a

> sorry leftover from that time. The machine was freshly cleaned and glowed. For almost every execution, I had new replacement parts. In front of hundreds of eyes – all the spectators stood on tiptoe right up to the hills there – the condemned man was laid down under the Harrow by the Commandant himself (Kafka 114-15).

According to John Frow, during the regime of the Old Commandant, executions were festivals to which crowds flocked to see Justice delivered. Children were given a privileged place near the apparatus to witness at the sixth hour the transfigured face of the suffering man. On the contrary, nobody attends executions these days. The machine is run down and the Officer can get no spare parts for it because the New Commandant disapproves of all that it represents. It becomes clear that the explorer is positioned in a struggle between the old and the new order (1-14).

Foucault analyses this political practice as it appears in the seventeenth century in *Discipline and Punish: The Birth of the Prison.* According to him, it is the engagement and interpretation of a witnessing audience that plays an essential part of the rhetorical situation in the representation of torture. Foucault writes, "today we are rather inclined to ignore it (public executions); perhaps, in its time, it gave rise to too much inflated rhetoric; perhaps it has been attributed too readily and too emphatically to a process of 'humanisation', thus dispensing with the need for further analysis"(7). The participation of the audience in producing the significance of torture is central to his study. He analyses the function of the audience in the persuasive effectiveness of torture witnessed and depicted. In the scenes of torture described in the ancient texts, the witness bears witness. The idea of bearing witness embodies both a legal and an ethical concept, both someone who observes and bears witness. The association of bodily pain with understanding "resonates from the ancient through the modern, within the idea of bearing witness" (Ballengee 6). The audience or witnesses observe a scene presented or represented before them, responds to the demands of the rhetoric, with an interpretation or judgment. Foucault's observation that the State demonstrates its power by inscribing on the bodies of its soldiers, prisoners, and civilians, is significant while reading it in the context of the penal society. The State displays its power through strategically placed bruises, wounds, and mutilations. The act of torture, or the results of torture that are presented to the public convey a message in a horrific manner similar to the execution procedure. The message stands for the unspoken word of the regime that inflicts torture and presents it as a spectacle. Torture, in many colonial regimes, served to make the victims confess the crimes they may or may not have committed through force. Confession, therefore, is another traumatic aspect of torture. In a manner, the relationship between torture, the tortured body, and the unspoken along with the intended meaning of the colonial regime work on the principle of confession. However, not only does this operate on the level of the confession of the victim, but also on the level of the witnessing public. The unspoken meaning is aimed at the audience who read the manifestations of torture, the intended meaning of the unspoken message.

As in its political context, the sight of a tortured body bears a non-linguistic meaning, where the painful inscriptions on the body inflict pain on the witnesses. Inscriptions might evoke a particular physical, intellectual, or emotional response in its reader or audience. Torture, be it in the real or the fictional worlds, communicates meaning that corresponds to the pain and trauma of witnessing the spectacle. In the literary and political scene of torture, the mutilated body must present before another or others, and the effectiveness of the same depends upon the response, of the one who witnesses the inscription on the tortured body. As Ballengee points out, "this witness may be the victim, the torturer, an observant bystander within the presented scene, or the audience of the event or "text" itself" (7). The events represented in literary texts by and large reflect on this dual nature of its witness: the witness or witnesses who are a part of the text-one who functions within the text, and the other who interacts from without-the reader. No matter what the case, torture is presented or staged in order to provoke a particular response from its witnesses. These responses of witnesses can vary between the dichotomies of apprehension and appreciation; the apprehension of the intended message evoked by the tortured body, or an appreciation of the intended message the tortured body conveys to the witnesses.

Through painful inscriptions, the body becomes an object. It becomes reduced to a bleeding mass as long as the torturer continues the inscription. The unbearable pain and suffering of the victim supposedly satiate the desire for order in the torturer. Subjecting the victim to intense pain might be the torturer's mode of ensuring the deliverance of justice and extraction of testimonies and confessions from the victim. Subject to excruciating pain, the nature of the victim's confessions and testimonies might be problematic. However, in Kafka, we see a victim who is entirely robbed of a testimony or a confession, set aside the credibility of the same.

Even though torture might not guarantee truthful testimonies and confessions, Elaine Scarry and others have theorised that the torturer continues to make use of torture to convey a general message of power to its victim thus "destroying the subjective world of the tortured and replacing it with the torturer's own ideology" (17). The "effectiveness" of torture lies in its ability to break down and eliminate all that is known and familiar, to deconstruct the intellect and rational, and to replace reason with unreason (8).

Torture and its attendant pain reinforce the notion of corporeality in the victim. The duration and intensity of torture have a similar effect on thc witness, at the level of bodily empathy. When we see a body in pain, it is with our bodies that we react. Witnessing torture sets forth traumatic memories in the witness as his/her body tells him/her of the experiences of pain and suffering that they might have endured or are about to go through. It reminds us the worst we have experienced and also makes us imagine the worst imaginable. It is in this bodily response, and also in the uncomfortable and gross consciousness of our bodies, that torture communicates the certainty of bodily awareness. Witnessing torture establishes an empathetic relationship between the victim and the witness which is not driven by logic.

Examine the case of Greek tragedies where bearing witness was a crucial aspect of participating in the tragedies. Ballengee discusses the Theban plays of Sophocles to establish the symbolic significance of the tortured body as a means of establishing social justice and judgment in medieval societies. Inflicting pain upon oneself was considered a means of achieving purgation. Torture and subsequent trauma were considered moral tools for paying the debt of trespassing law and legal structures. Punishment, and its performance in front of an anticipating, witnessing citizenry further resolve the pollution and tension created by a crime. The motif of the tortured body, as well as the theme of torture, pain and trauma is rampant throughout ancient literature. Adding to the effect was the nature of the theatrical performance of the plays. The texts in itself accommodated a set of witnesses bearing witness to the act of torture and trauma, further performed in front of another group of witnesses, the actual audience. It is the actual audience who are truly affected by the trauma.

To judge people of the past with the morality of our times would be fallacious. People routinely exposed to pain would hold different attitudes regarding human suffering. In earlier times, executing somebody behind closed doors was regarded nothing less than murder as this derived the victim of a final chance from meeting a crowd, and deliver a final speech, and was crucial to the State or power structure to parade their authority to those who fall under its jurisdiction. The lethal injection, introduced in 1977, is considered today's most humane method of execution. Neither painless nor dignified, death by lethal injection is still not a private affair with so many people watching over needles injecting poisonous compounds into a person's bloodstream.

Analysing trauma in memorial cultures is in itself a trauma. This is because memorialisation is characterised by the privileging of the notion of witnessing with its constraints on comprehension and representation. Witnesses need not resolve conflicts and problems of the past, but they do offer diverse perspectives to look at history. Every witness is a door that leads to different corridors, and every corridor leads to different rooms and readings. There is a gap between what one sees and what one writes because of the influence of trauma that the witness knowingly or unknowingly is subjected to. Every witness is, in that sense, a victim of trauma, unable to comprehend and recreate what had happened right in front of their eyes or the experience he/she has gone through while watching the same. How witnesses are affected by traumatic situations is different. In, *In the Penal Colony*, Kafka presents situations and people who are not centuries apart from one another but experience the opposite of what each other felt at the sight of a condemned penalised by the killing apparatus. The civil celebration of the past is set against a sense of contempt for torture in the present.

The Officer and the traveler express an essential conflict about their view of the world. The traveler rejects approval for the continuing usage of the apparatus and its execution power. The European traveler, who was fundamentally opposed to any kind of death penalty, and this kind of mechanical style, in particular, is accused of being trapped in the European kind of thinking as observed by the Officer. The fact that the history of Europe is stained in the blood of countless victims of blood-chilling public executions is an irony in itself. As Steph Craps points out, the Eurocentric understanding of trauma is in itself flawed as it considers Europe to be a trauma-free zone and fails to take into account the trauma-driven British imperialism that happened and continue to happen (4). The traveler, who was certain that the system of justice and the apparatus in the isolated and self-contained penal colony were unjust and inhumane, did however prevent the execution of the helpless man. This exhibits his double standards on humanity and compassion towards a fellow being. Kafka tears apart the European mask of human values.

In the Penal Colony occupies a unique place in Kafka's works as it describes a collective trauma that takes place in a colonialist, totalitarian regime. With its graphic violence and the pedantic detached manner of the description of the torture mechanism, Kafka's classic piece, is a nerve-racking reminder of how humanity has accustomed themselves to the very idea of humiliation, torture, and trauma, without bearing a slight grain of regret. The tale has attracted a range of critical approaches, ranging from cultural-historical readings via post-colonial approaches to deconstruction. The narrative is structured around the opposition between the enlightened Western traveler and the strange rituals of an exotic society. However, the penal colonies were indeed a European creation, and the torture machine symbolic of modern technology and human progress at its most advanced and destructive. The killing machine's victim has external witnesses to the physicality of his trauma. However, his real trauma and torment exists inside, as he is the only one who can understand it. Even if given an opportunity to speak about their trauma to others, these victims would have a hard time as the issues they faced were unnatural and dehumanising. Being left with no chance of survival, the trauma of Kafka's victims dies with them, unsaid and unheard.

Literature carries us through a process of identification with the experiences of both the victim and the perpetrator. The challenge of depicting torture and trauma in literature indeed conforms to our capacity to bear, tolerate, and witness. As readers, we have the double responsibility of hearing through the silence and unheard voices of the victims while also identifying the stench of raw blood and taste of hatred in the perpetrator's mouth. Analysing trauma, in other words, depends on our capacity to bear witness to and understand trauma.

Works Cited

"Diary Entries from October 1660", *The Diary of Samuel Pepys: Daily Entries from the 17th Century London Diary*, 6 Dec. 2020, pepysdiary.com/diary/1660/10/.

Adelmann, Rebecca A, editor. "Review of Gestures of Gestures of Testimony: Torture, Trauma, and Affect in Literature" Michael Richardson. *Cultural Studies*, vol. 31, no. 5, 2017.

Balaev, Michelle, editor. *Contemporary Approaches in Literary Trauma Theory*. Palgrave, 2014.

Ballengee, Jennifer R. *The Wound and the Witness: The Rhetoric of Torture*. SUNY P, 2009.

Blakemore, Eric. "Why the Nazis Were Obsessed With Twins: Horrifying medical experiments on twins helped Nazis justify the Holocaust". *History*. 8 July 2019, history.com/news/nazi-twin-experiments-mengele-eugenics. .

Breuer, Josef and Sigmund Freud. Studies on Hysteria. Basic Books, 2009.

Caruth, Cathy, editor. *Trauma: Explorations in Memory*. Johns Hopkins UP, 1995.

.... *Unclaimed Experience: Trauma*, Narrative, and History. Johns Hopkins UP, 1996.

Craps, Steph. *Postcolonial Witnessing: Trauma Out of Bounds*. Palgrave MacMillan, 2013

Felman, Shoshana. *The Juridical Unconscious: Trials and Traumas in the Twentieth Century*. Harvard UP, 2002.

Foucault, Michel. *Discipline and Punish: The Birth of the Prison*. Translated by Alan Sheridan, Vintage, 1977.

Freud, Sigmund. *Beyond The Pleasure Principle*. Translated by James Strachey, W. W. Norton & Company, 1961.

Frow, John. "In the Penal Colony". *Australian Humanities Review*, April, 1999.

Kafka, Franz. "In the Penal Colony." *Greatest Works: Franz Kafka*. Maple, 2013, p.p. 96-134.

Nietzsche, Friedrich W. *The Gay Science*. Translated by Thomas Common. Dover Publications, 2006.

Politzer, Heinz. *Franz Kafka: Parable and Paradox*. Cornell, 1962.

Richardson, Michael. *Gestures of Testimony: Torture, Trauma, and Affect in Literature*. Bloomsbury Academic, 2016.

Ryan, Perry T. *The Last Public Execution in America*. Kentucky, 1992.

Sans, Silvia Amati. "Ambiguity as a Defence in Extreme Trauma". *Bearing Witness: Psychoanalytic Work with People Traumatised by Torture and State Violence*. Gautier, Andres and Anna Sabatini Scalmati. Karac, 2010.

Scarry, Elaine. *The Body in Pain: The Making and Unmaking of the World*. Oxford UP, 1985.

Skoda, Hannah. "Torture and Brutality in Medieval Literature – By Larissa Tracy." *History: The Journal of the Historical Association*, vol. 334, 2014, p. 121.

Tracy, Larrisa. *Torture and Brutality in Medieval Literature: Negotiations of National Identity*. D. S. Brewer, 2012.

Welch, Megan. "Torture and Brutality in Medieval Literature." *Journal of Religious History*, vol. 38, no. 4, Dec. 2014, pp. 604-605.

CHAPTER 8

History, Memory and Testimony: Gendered Victimhood and Post Traumatic Vulnerability in Suroopa Mukherjee's *Surviving Bhopal*

Navya Chandran

Suroopa Mukherjee's *Surviving Bhopal* attempts to comprehend the cultural memory of Bhopal gas victims through a thorough study of their oral testimony underpinned with documents such as newspapers, archives, pictures and monuments. Cultural memory is defined as "the characteristic store of repeatedly used texts, images and rituals in the cultivation of which each society and epoch stabilises and imports its self-image; a collectively shared knowledge of preferably (yet no exclusively) the past, on which a group bases its awareness of unity and character" (Assmann 15). Selection of memories from the past is a highly unscientific process, referring to how a victim chooses to remember the past and reinterpret certain events determines only his/her version of truth. Mukherjee's focus is on the gendered victimisation of women in Bhopal whose memories of the day of disaster constitute the foundation of Bhopal's cultural memory.

Maria Duffy in her work *Paul Ricoeur's Pedagogy of Pardon: A Narrative Theory of Memory and Forgetting,* describes how memory is structured in culture, civic identity and even religion and how it can be used as an effective tool to help resolve and heal past wounds. As a first step in explaining his theory of memory, Ricoeur distinguishes between two dimensions of memory – first one is cognitive whereas the second one pragmatic which corresponds roughly to the Greek notion of mneme and anamnesis (258). Anamnesis is the act of remembering a memory from the past as a culmination of a set of recollections, which is basically an individual's version of truth. His book focuses on the importance of confronting problematic pasts in order to prevent future victim trauma that is associated with the disaster. Ricoeur calls the suffering community to engage in the past critically, to risk a dynamic narrative exploration and ultimately work towards reconciliation.

According to Mukherjee, the most distinctive feature of Bhopali women is their willingness to talk about the night of the disaster and its immediate consequences and how it affected them specifically being in a position of double marginalisation. She ropes in women who had firsthand experience of the Bhopal gas tragedy, records their narratives, helps them to come to terms with their troubled past and slowly focus on the future ahead of them. The tone is not that of sympathy, Mukherjee in fact condemns the bizarre media generated images of Bhopal. She recognises women in Bhopal to be stronger than men when it comes to facing adversities in life. They realise the need for constant help from external sources to bring about an improvement in their plight and hence they are vocal about their problems.

While recording the eye witness accounts of Bhopali women about the night of the industrial disaster, Mukherjee recognises the most prominent image in all those oral narrativesas the image of people running (47). Later the images of death began to dissipate followed by other more compelling images. The plethora of images of women aborting as they run, fetuses kept in laboratory bottles, monstrous births, mother cradling a deformed child and organochlorines in the breast milk of mothers, to suggest a few. But Mukherjee shifts the focus from women being in a position of permanent victimisation to women who are busy fighting a daily struggle for survival.

As she observes: Bhopali women were able to utilise the disadvantages as tools for their struggle. They developed what can be best described as a self-help kit. The tools were innovativeness, self-reliance, sense of solidarity and healthy contempt for official channels of power and bureaucratic systems (58). These women invaded public spaces and used people's power as strong weapon. Feisty, gallant and fearless they raised their voices in order to be heard. Therefore, it is not at all surprising that Bhopali women use their stories as tools of empowerment. In the process they have made one thing very clear that Bhopal may have lost its status as a 'headline event' but the questions that were raised as early as the morning after the disaster still continues to be relevant.

Retelling catastrophic events from the past is inevitably traumatic. The trauma narrative is a psychological technique used to help survivors of trauma make sense of their experience, while also acting as a form of exposure to painful memories. Trauma stories are organically shared through verbal, written or artistic means, thus allowing the individual to organise their memories and coming to terms with the pain they are destined to live with. In his article "After Bhopal" that appears in *Unheard Voices: Stories of Forgotten Times*, Harsh Mander highlights community mental health activities and intervention research as the most immediate need in Bhopal (10). To bring out the contemporary reality of the mentally distressed survivor groups, he studies them categorically and registers first hand experiences of trauma faced by the victims in his article. Mander describes the case of Sunil who was 11 years old at the time of disaster, he was left with his younger brother and sister to cut across his path of survival. He survived the tragedy, but it took a toll on the growing child's mind. Mander notes:

> As time passed, Sunil became more and more withdrawn and uncommunicative. Slowly, almost imperceptibly, he found something cracking up within him. He was frequently depressed, and became obsessed by the thoughts of suicide. He heard voices call out to him. He would not stir out of his home, would not wash himself or talk to people. The neighbours took care of his brother and sister and fed Sunil... There were times when he ran out of the house without clothes. Feverishly roaming on streets night and day, running for kilometres on the railway track into the forest (11).

Suroopa Mukherjee's *Surviving Bhopal* explores the lives of thousands of female victims through their stories, told orally, and records them to recognise what life was to them in the three decades after the disaster. Mukherjee works on similar lines with Mander, only difference being the shift of focus from male to female gender through the incorporation of a broader canvas that brings in images, texts and oral testimonials drawn from 'archival sources, fieldwork and secondary material'(2). The book hence treads a middle ground between the dry, inaccessible, government – sponsored documents about Bhopal Gas Tragedy and the highly commercialised media and magazine stories to bring about a more credible and acceptable narration of the real story. Mukherjee takes it upon herself the task of writing about the 'historical wound' (8), the understanding of alternative, forgotten histories. The recovery and regeneration of such histories are done by closely studying a range of institutions that are "not historiographical in nature but memorial, literary, filmic, therapeutic and quasilegal" (78).

The identification of actual victim position in the wake of any tragedy is an absolute necessity. To define the victims in Bhopal tragedy, the comprehensive understanding of its history is important. Bhopal Gas Tragedy is recognised universally as one among the worst manmade disaster, often compared to the collapse of RMS Titanic or reactor explosion in Chernobyl. On December 3, 1984, more than 40 tons of Methyl isocyanate gas leaked from pesticide plant of Union Carbide India Limited (UCIL), a subsidiary of the America based company Union Carbide Cooperation (UCC). In "The Bhopal disaster and its aftermath: A review", Edward Broughton states:

> The incident immediately killed 3,800 people, causing significant morbidity and premature death of many thousand more. The company involved in what became the worst industrial accident in history immediately tried to dissociate itself from legal responsibility. Eventually it reached a settlement with the Indian government through mediation of that country's Supreme Court and accepted moral responsibility. It paid $470 million in compensation, a relatively small amount based on significant underestimations of long-term health consequences of exposure and the number of people exposed (6).

The area built and developed by Nawabs of Bhopal who reigned during early eighteenth century is commonly known as Old City. The government offices, ministers' bungalows and residential areas of richer section of society lived in the Central part. The South had Industrial Township catering to government-run engineering industries. At the wake of Bhopal Gas Tragedy, only people in Old City were affected. A large section of them were immigrant workers, who migrated to Bhopal looking for better job prospects but ended up being daily wage workers providing physical labour.

The insidious nature of the gas leak, spreading late at night through the air into poorly constructed homes, to lakhs of people who were sleeping, led to a situation where they had no chance to escape, to take preventive measures or even alarm others who were yet to encounter the massive gas leak. Even after 36 years of the disaster, no effective measures have been taken for the redressal of the victims. Years of neglect and humiliation increases the need for bringing in media attention to the current scenario amidst hearsay, rumours and exaggerations. As a matter of fact, David Weir coined the phrase "Bhopal Syndrome" to show that Bhopal remains a blot on the forward march of the civilisation, simply because it represented what was "fundamentally wrong in our stewardship of the world" (Weir 1985).

Mukherjee identifies the women community living in Old City as those who belonged to the minority Muslim community and did piece – rate work from inside their homes, who lived lives in purdah within the strict confinement of their families. So, the "victim" category during Bhopal Gas Tragedy is this small group of under privileged daily wage workers and their family who lived in Old City, away from the elite class of Bhopal. Their sense of trauma arises from the sudden inexplicable tragic experience that was left unaccounted for over many decades. The sense of doom and disappointment was transferred from one generation to the next, along with the physical and clinical deformities that came with the disastrous gas leak. Mukherjee dedicates the book to the 'wounded generation... the children of Bhopal survivors' (*Surviving Bhopal* ix).

Immediately after the disaster, two types of testimonials were actively generated – one by the victim-survivor groups and other by the mainstream social media. The victim testimonials had a target audience in mind, in was mainly intended to lead to some activism. Media testimonials highlighted human-interest stories to evoke middle class responses. In this case both the testimonials are flawed and rejected by Mukherjee. Briefly looking at the kind of oral testimonials used in the book, it is mainly of two types – one from the archival sources and another from live interviews. Mukherjee aims at the imaginative reconstruction of the tragedy through processes of remembering, forgetting filtering the truth, emphasis, recalling and trying to make sense of things that becomes part of telling (43). Individual and collective memories are used in a way that places individual stories in a wider context of socio-economic and political background. The testimonials are gender specific in that they capture women's voices, though the male voice is brought to give comparative perspective. The narratives are drawn from different age groups, given their strategic positioning on the night of the disaster and how they survived to tell their tales.

It was Sigmund Freud who first theorised trauma in relation historical violence, mainly in the context of World War I and World War II. His ideas can be mainly found in two of his books – *Beyond Pleasure Principle* and *Moses and Monotheism.* Freud observed the pathological condition that followed the World Wars – psychic disorders that had deep roots in the imposition of tragic historic events in the past. Freud calls this mental state as the accident neurosis. It is characterised by repetitive intrusion of nightmares and reliving of events that happened the night of disaster.

In his work *Moses and Monotheism*, Freudsuggests that even if one gets away apparently unharmed from the spot of disaster, in the following weeks, he/she will develop a series of grave physical and motor symptoms which can be ascribed only to his shock or whatever else happened at the time of the accident. The time gap between the disaster and the appearance of the symptoms for the first time is called the incubation period. In her work *Unclaimed Experiences*, Cathy Caruth quotes Freud who tried to explain how certain individuals who had to go through catastrophic events in the past, tend to live with a peculiar pattern of suffering throughout their life. In Freud's text, trauma is understood as a wound inflicted not upon the body but upon the mind. It is studied under the combined term post-traumatic stress disorder or PTSD. So, what was considered a single violent original event in the individual's past slowly acts as a vantage point to accumulate further insecurities and manifests itself in the form of nightmares or repetitive actions of the survivor appearing from time to time. As Caruth observes:

> Trauma describes an overwhelming experience of sudden or catastrophic events in which the response to the event occurs in the often delayed, uncontrolled repetitive appearances of hallucinations and other intrusive phenomena... trauma seems to be much more than a pathology or the simple illness of a wounded psyche: it is always the story of a wound that cries out, that addresses us in the attempt to tell us of a reality or truth that is not otherwise available. This truth, in its delayed appearance and its belated address, cannot be linked only to what is known, but also to what remains unknown in our very actions and our language (11).

Psychiatry, psychoanalysis and neurobiology are three different streams that directly insisted on the effects of external violence in psychic disorders. As the dialogue goes in the movie *The Pawnbroker* –

- What happened?
- Happened?
- Yes.
- I didn't die.

This painful repetition of the flashback can only be understood as the absolute inability of the mind to avoid an unpleasurable event that has not been given psychic meaning in any way. In the case of accident neurosis, the outside has gone inside without any mediation. The only way to deal with this state of affairs is to find a cathartic outlet for the distressing emotions. Narrating traumatic incidents helps individuals to deal with complex and multiple traumas. The process of contextualising traumatic experiences and studying them as experienced by the victims is understood under the broad term Narrative Exposure Therapy (NET). It is one of the most used remedy in community settings when individuals experience trauma as a result of political, cultural or social forces.

Preserving the memory of a highly disastrous, tragic and disruptive event in a nation's contemporary history is a highly political act. In a process of recollecting what happened at the night of the disaster almost three decades back, different memories can be taken into account – complied and compared to make sense of the event in its entirety. For the last 30 years, the State remembers Bhopal only on its anniversary day, which is demonstrated by a two-minute silence in the legislative assembly. In their article "Remembering Bhopal: Voices of Survivors", Rama Lakshmi and Shalini Sharma observe:

> The survivor groups claim a moral right to their memory and have consistently demanded that they should be involved in creating a living memorial to the disaster that informs present and future generations about the worst cooperate massacre in world history. Much like "memory-communities" that have kept the Holocaust stories alive and uninterrupted the survivors of Bhopal will provide testimonials and curate and construct the memorial/museum. If only the survivors in Bhopal have the moral right to remember and preserve their story, then any official or even academic attempt to usurp it will rob it off its raw energy. For the struggle of justice that is still alive on the streets of Bhopal, the story is not wrapped and does not have a neat ending (30).

The impact of trauma often differs for men and women. Women are more likely to feel traumatic events more intensely and respond to it until they develop Post Traumatic Stress Disorder. Ehlers and Clarkmetaphorically describe traumatic memory as a cupboard in which many things have been thrown in quickly and in a disorganised fashion. Rather, the memory is disorganised and incoherent, consisting of 'items' scattered around as well as some are missing, hampering the construction of a clear, coherent narrative. The inability to voluntarily retrieve and describe trauma memory in an organised and coherent fashion is called fragmentation (Van der Kolk and Fisler, 1995). An attempt to preserve the original event through the study of memory of some female survivor community is seen in Mukherjee's Surviving Bhopal.

The testimonies in the book gives an insight into the lives of three main women, Aziza – who is a community health worker, Rashida Bi – President of Bhopal Gas PeeditMahila Stationary Karamchari Sangh (BGPMSKS) her account of how she learnt to live through the aftermath by fighting for her rights, Champa Devi Shukla – secretary of BGPMSKS, talks about the pain and suffering of a woman who is the sole bread-winner of the family whose second generation is also affected and finally Satinath Sarangi who describes his role as "support from outside, to the people's movement". Satinath (commonly referred in the book as Sathyu) is a member of the privileged middle class, who have not been exposed to the toxic gas thus an outsider to the victim community. But he belongs to Bhopal Group for Information and Action (BGIA), which is a voluntary group of thinkers, professionals, writers, researchers and activists with worldwide affiliations. Aziza provides the memory of the event, Rashida Bi and Champa Devi gives an insight to the modes of practice, while Sathyu gives a broader theoretical perspective.

During the time of tragedy, Aziza was a young mother with two children and she was pregnant with the third. On the night of the gas leak, her husband was away in Jaipur for work and through her poorly constructed pucca house the gas oozed in like "insidious white cloud creeping in stealthily through the gaps and filling the room" (*Dancing on the Streets* 169). Aziza recollects how her daughter and mother-in-law chocked and coughed continuously after inhaling the gas. In her words "each breath they took seared their throats as though they were breathing fire. Their eyes burned as if red chilly powder had been rubbed into them and outside her house, she could listen to people screaming and shouting 'Bhago, Bhago' (*Dancing on the Streets* 170). Any narration about the night of the disaster has a similar frame.

The initial shock was rooted in the fact that the gas leak was inexplicable in its dimensions. Aziza and her family left their home in their clothes they wore for bed because they had to get away somehow to escape the situation. They did not lock their house. Aziza's feels guilty about not being able to help her near and dear ones. She held her children closely and ran towards Hamidia hospital whereas her father-in-law climbed into a truck loaded with people because he was stronger than the rest. He tried to pull his favourite grandson (Aziza's sister-in-law's son) into the truck, but in that confusion, he caught the hand of another boy who was running beside him. Such choices were hard to make, especially when it comes to saving the lives of one's loved ones. As Rashida Bi points out "when mothers are compelled to abandon their crying children because they can pick up only one or two, then you know you are witnessing the end of the world" (*Dancing in the Streets* 174)

The sights immediately after the disaster was terrifying with dead bodies lying all over the ground stripped of all human dignity. Some of them were merely unconscious but no one bothered to check them anyway. The smell of vomit, faeces and blood filled the air. Many of them had deserted the place with whatever little they could get hold of. The poorest of the poor, women and children were left in Bhopal Old town to die. Women like Rashida Bi who were born in traditional orthodox Muslim families were confined to live inside their houses from a very early age and received no formal education. They did menial jobs and earned little money to support the family and wore purdah all her life. In the wake of a disaster, they were doubly marginalised – they suffered at the hands of patriarchy, social oppression, denial of human rights and on top of all that the gas attack.

In her article "Dancing in the streets: Narratives of resistance in Bhopal" eighteen years after the gas tragedy, Suroopa Mukherjee quotes the narrative of Champa Devi,

> We were all running in different directions, but we tried to stay together as a family. My husband worked as a labourer in an agricultural workshop. He was not able to run a great distance. He fell in a heap on the wayside and injured himself badly. For the next few days, he began passing blood in his urine. The fall had permanently damaged his kidneys. He remained continuously ill till his death in 1997. He suffered from deep depression because the gas had rendered him unemployable, and it hurt his sense of manhood that he could not provide for his family. My granddaughter was born with a missing palate and cleft lip (172).

In his book *Writing History, Writing Trauma*, Dominick LaCapra states that there are two fundamental forms of remembering traumatic events – "acting out" and "working through" (41). He was precisely applying the theories in psychoanalysis to historical studies. In "acting out", one compulsively relives the traumatic events of the past in the present. Whereas in "working through"(42), the victim tries to distinguish between the experience that traumatised him/her and his/her present life. A person who tries to "work through" is never wholly trapped in the past. For women like Champa Devi, narrating the events during the night of disaster is the only way she can make sense of what happened with her life. She represents people who use their memories in a deliberate and conscious effort to make sense of the mammoth process of "containing" and "controlling" what followed the disaster. It can be considered as a form of Narrative Exposure Therapy. "What gives the testimonials its particular emotive power is that survivors do not flinch from giving graphic details. Despite the fact that the process of remembering has been painful. Time is a healer, the popular adage assures us, but in the case of Bhopal, the passage of time has only sharpened the pain, making memories more volatile" says Mukherjee (47).

The medical conditions of the victims of the tragedy were highly unpredictable and bizarre. Some of them developed conditions that were unknown to the medical world before and the most affected group was the children. Mukherjee adds the narrative of Razia Bi:

> My three-year-old daughter Nazma had swollen up so much like she would burst. We took her to Hamidia Hospital. We stayed with her in the hospital for fifteen days and then the doctors said she would not survive. We were feeling so helpless because there was no doctor around who knew how my baby could be saved. She died on the fifteenth day (50).

She also adds the narrative of Zubeda Bi:

> My grandson was one year old then. I put him on my chest to protect him as much as possible. But his face swelled to twice its size, his eyes were puffed tight. We were really scared (50).

In an industrial disaster, the course of things gets damaged permanently because it takes a toll on the emotional well-being of the victims. It is an irrecuperable damage that affects generations. The United Nations Department of Humanitarian Affairs defines disaster as a serious disruption of the functioning of society, causing widespread human, material or environmental losses which exceed the ability of affected society to cope on its own resources. Allen W. Batteau's article "Aggressive technology in a century of Industrial disasters" states that "what distinguishes a disaster from an accident is this: accidents and natural events such as hurricanes and earthquakes claim life and damage property, but disasters damage, sometimes fatally, entire communities, industrial and political regimes" (28).

When Sathyu visits Bhopal before the disaster as a part of her work in the research laboratory, he finds out problems regarding the backwardness in industrial sector in Bhopal. The state government and the UCIL were neglectful about the necessity of strict safety precautions and need for community awareness. After the gas leak, the affected category was the migrant labour class population who lived in the margin of the city in fast mushrooming, illegal localities. It was a hard task to organise these random group of people into activism in the wake of the disaster because they had very little experience in collective movements. Their demands were basic – shelter, clean drinking water, increased job opportunities and medical care. The activist groups were later taken up by political parties whose leaders never belonged to the victim category, hence unaware of the extent of distress. Thus, activism slowly waded away leaving the victims no hope for an upcoming brighter future.

The Bhopal Gas PeeditMahila Stationary Karamchari Sangh (BGPMSKS) is one of the 40 'yojanas' initiated by the government for rehabilitation of Gas tragedy victims. They are entrusted with various jobs like weaving, tailoring, making stationary products for government offices etc, but most of them were struggling with lack of empathy from the government's side. Their working place was something like a big hall with piled up papers and outdated machinery. They were viewed as a collective of women with the potential to turn against the government and make trouble. So, they were not given any privileges so that all they would want to think about is filling their empty stomachs.

Bhopal Group for Information and Action (BGIA) was formed in 1986 to work with the propaganda of bringing in active people outside the community to speak for the victims. Accurate information regarding the situation was collected and action plans were generated. They kept themselves away from party politics that worked with the sole aim of recruiting people into political parties. The action plan of BGIA was more humane. Government yojanas like BGPMSKS associated with BGIA for support and instructions to work for progress.

One of the key factors that these organisationsemphasised on is 'Mahila Power.' Women who are doubly marginalised have problems specific to them and in can only be articulated by a 'Mahila' or woman. Men who tried to leaders of these resistance groups, with previous experience of being group leaders, who are articulate and bold, soon lost interest and faded away. It was women who persisted. In her interview with Sathyu, Mukherjee learns that their aim is to be present in the social, political and cultural spaces so that they won't be forgotten. They are trying desperately to make their presence known in a world that constantly wants to forget them. To quote Terry Allan's poem:

> We are women of Bhopal we are flames not flowers
> We will not wilt before you cooperate power
> With our blooms in hand we're gonna sweep you away
> Cause we will fight for our justice till our dyin' day ("Flames not Flowers")

About the emergence of protest against authorities in Bhopal, Mukherjee observes that "It was confrontation with lies almost daily that first started the stirrings of protest. The women I spoke to look back with hindsight at the growing consciousness of having been wronged by a system. They all tell me that it was women who shifted away from their personal sufferings to the need for collective action" (55). Agencies like BGPMSKS and BGIA were efforts from women folk in Bhopal to address their issues which they thought, would never be conveyed accurately by any political party led by men. In addition to this, women also engaged themselves in providing care within the family, along with the additional burden of working in a largely conflict-ridden and administratively mismanaged workplace.

Despite constant protests, marches and outcry to bring media and government attention to the case of their marginalisation, they have not achieved anything fundamental ever after three decades of activism. So, people affected by the gas leak remains as a highly segregated group with babies born with strange deformities, odd death patterns, impotent men, poor jobless women and no basic facilities to move on with their daily life. Remembering the incident is largely confined to the yearly demonstrations on the day of the disaster and empty shacks that once protested against the company and government demanding their fundamental rights.

The focus of Mukherjee is in the long-lasting aftereffects of the tragedy, quite different from the media generated images of the disaster – mostly faces of men and women staring blankly at an uncertain future. Despite being world's worst manmade disaster, it has gone through a saga of neglect, firstly with the failure in proper documentation and lack of authentic data and secondly failure in including the study of it in medical, disaster management or other study circles. Unknown to the mainstream academic and research circles, local efforts have gone into collecting indigenous material – records of newspaper clippings, campaign materials, press releases and so on, which is later stored by offices of survivors. In addition to this, there was a radical attempt to deconstruct the existing "truth" and "reality" by interpreting the oral narratives of women to create a more inclusive and fully human conception of social reality.

Mukherjee's aim in writing the book was to take up the task of "uncovering true facts to pierce the veil of secrecy that gave impunity to those responsible for the tragedy" (Mukherjee 3). In the decades long struggle none of the demands – good health, toxic-free environment, right to information, right to a life of dignity – has been adequately met. The implicit suggestion in the title about 'surviving' in Bhopal rather than 'living' in it suggests a political question about the state of affairs in Bhopal almost after 36 years of the tragedy. A disastrous event like Bhopal Gas Tragedy inevitably scars the victim, its residues leaving him/her permanently weakened in the face of a future stress. Mukherjee demonstrates how narrative exposure therapy can be used as an active tool to deal with troubled past. She uses resources provided by oral history by women, to recreate the interface between what is reported officially and the lived experience of trauma and suffering as recorded through the neglected voices of people. Analysing the eye witness accounts by women brings into light their double marginalisation and gendered victimhood. She has successfully addressed the emotional, cognitive, behavioural and physical damages that followed the disaster with specific reference given to the redefined gendered victim category.

Works Cited

Allen, Terry. "Flames Not Flowers." (2004). *Movement in Motion*, 2020, movementinmotion.bandcamp.com/.

Assmann, Jan. *Cultural Memory and Early Civilisation: Writing, Remembrance, and Political Imagination*. Cambridge University Press, 2011.

Batteau, Allen. "Aggressive Technology in a Century of Industrial Disasters." *Practicing Anthropology*, vol. 23, no. 4, 2001, pp. 28–32., doi:10.17730/praa.23.4.p46445vr754r2507.

Broughton, Edward. "The Bhopal Disaster and Its Aftermath: A Review." *Environmental Health*, vol. 4, no. 1, 2005, doi:10.1186/1476-069x-4-6.

Caruth, Cathy. *Unclaimed Experience: Trauma, Narrative, and History*. Johns Hopkins UP, 2016.

Duffy, Maria. *Paul Ricoeur's Pedagogy of Pardon: A Narrative Theory of Memory and Forgetting*. Continuum, 2012.

Freud, Sigmund, et al. *Beyond the Pleasure Principle and Other Writings*. Penguin Books, 2003.

.... *Moses and Monotheism*. Translated by Katherine Jones, Vintage Books, 1967.

Kolk, Bessel A. Van Der, and Rita Fisler. "Dissociation and the Fragmentary Nature of Traumatic Memories: Overview and Exploratory Study." *Journal of Traumatic Stress*, vol. 8, no. 4, 1995, pp. 505–525., doi:10.1002/jts.2490080402.

LaCapra, Dominick. *Writing History, Writing Trauma*. The Johns Hopkins UP, 2014.

Lakshmi, Rama, and Shalini Sharma. "Remembering Bhopal: Voices of Survivors." *Social Justice*, vol. 41, 2014, pp. 28–37.

Mander, Harsh. *Unheard Voices: Stories of Forgotten Lives*. Penguin Books, 2001.

Mukherjee, Suroopa. "'Dancing in the Streets': Protest, Celebration, and Modes of Self-Expression." *Surviving Bhopal*, 2010, pp. 159–184., doi:10.1057/9780230106321_8.

.... Surviving Bhopal: Dancing Bodies, Written Texts, and Oral Testimonials of Women in the Wake of an Industrial Disaster. Palgrave Macmillan, 2010.

The Pawnbroker. Directed by Sidney Lumet, Landau Company, 1964.

Weir, David. *The Bhopal Syndrome: Pesticides, Environment and Health*. Sierra Club Books, 1988.

CHAPTER 9

'The Unkindest Cut': Female Genital Mutilation in Alice Walker's *Possessing the Secret of Joy*

Indu V. Nandakumar and Geethu V. Nandakumar

Conceptual discourses on culture and the labyrinths of power dynamics in cultural systems are as old as the genesis of anthropological and cultural studies. A study on a specific society necessarily falls into the study of its cultural aspects and the various ways in which it gets manifested. A society is an amalgamation of individuals organised in structured social relationship according to a unique culture. Though the general notion about the term associates it to the higher order of human mind such as art, literature, music, painting etc., it has much wider significations, for it reflects the ways of the life of the members of society, or of group within a society. Culture forms the base of all human activities – the beliefs that create religion, traditional practices, power structures, gender constructs and the myriad of things associated with it.

Culture thus becomes the collective name for very solid patterns of beliefs, thoughts, traditions, values and practices. These are handed down from one generation to the other to warrant the continuity of these systems. Pertaining to one's culture gives its members a sense of identity and belonging which is an important aspect of social life. The perpetuation of culture takes place largely through the socialisation of its members and the various agencies like religion, Patriarchy, family and institutions play an active role in this process especially in the performitivity of its female subjects. The weight of culture is so tremendous that one does not escape the psychological conditioning even with migration.

The gender of 'woman' as a whole is controlled and dominated by the so called 'patriarchy' and customs from the very beginning of the days when people began to live as communities. The range of suppression of women may vary depending upon the difference in region and culture. Yet such characteristics like the control over women's sexuality, mobility and her right over her body cuts across class, caste, ethnicity, regions and religions. This restriction has a historical growth and is further institutionalised and legitimised by several ideologies, social structures and practices perpetuated through different cultural agencies like family, religion, caste, education, media, law, state and society. The socialising agencies play a key role in conditioning the women into appropriate behaviours and accepted norms of the society for they believe that in a woman's honour and virginity/chastity rests the pride of a nation, a clan or a family. Thus, disciplining the female body through various cultural practices becomes crucial concerns in a patriarchal society. Many of the practices portrayed as part of culture or religion which impinge on human rights, such as the notion of monogamy at the lowest level and harmful cultural practices at a higher level, with the attendant female subordination and domestication, are gender specific and they preserve patriarchy at the expense of women's rights.

Immense importance laid down on the culture often blinds one to the violation of human rights which takes place in the guise of specific practices. A number of such practices are harmful to the physical as well as psychological health of the individual, especially women and children. Some of them bring in excruciating physical pain while others subject them to humiliating and degrading treatment. These practices often stem out of entrenched discriminatory views about the status of women in the society. They maintain the subordination of women in society and legitimize and perpetuate gender-based violence reducing women to subhuman assets belonging to men. Various forms of gender-based violence like rape, incest, marital rape, enforced sterilisation etchas been regarded by the feminists as one of the most pervasive of human rights violations, denying women and girls' equality, security, dignity, self-worth, and their right to enjoy fundamental freedoms. Such violence is highly rampant within the family, remains widely socially tolerated and is often a cycle of abuse that manifests itself in an endless variety of forms. In addition to this, gross amount of gendered violence takes place over women's body through certain "harmful cultural practices" like Female Genital Mutilation, Chinese Foot binding, Corsetry, Breast Ironing to name a few. Susan Bordo argues in her book *Unbearable Weight, Feminism, Western Culture and the Body* that these practices are meant to train the female body in docility and obedience to cultural demands while at the same time being experienced in terms of 'power' and 'control' (20). Though the veracity of these cultural practices is being rationally challenged, and the need to wipe away many of these exerted, the dominant power believes in a faulty static, essentialist and holistic concept of culture which they argue is a hurdle to overcome.

Female Genital Mutilation has been such a cultural marker in countries of Africa and many other parts of the world and still continues to showcase the cultural heritage of those people. The Fact Sheet of WHO defines it as a process that involves "the partial or total removal of external female genitalia or other injury to the female genital organs for non-medical reasons" (1). One of the most profound values relating to FGM is 'purity'. The basic rationale for FGM in many practising communities is that it makes the girl child 'pure', so she can emerge into adulthood ready for the economic transaction which will result in her early marriage, and cleansed of the genital organs which are regarded as unclean, perhaps taboo. FGM is in many ways the ultimate sickening patriarchal oppression and a calculated practice stemmed out of an incoherent fear of female sexuality.

There are an estimated 130 million girls and women alive today whose human rights have been violated by this barbaric practice. This affects not only girls and women in Africa and the Middle East where it is traditionally practised, but also touches the lives and health of hundreds of women and girls living in migrant communities in industrialised countries including UK, Western Europe and countries such as US, Canada and Australia. Though FGM takes different forms and are manifested in different ways in different cultures, it can undoubtedly be called as a gross violation of human rights. The United Nations "Intergency statement on ending FGM" states that Female Genital Mutilation violates a series of well-established human rights principles, norms and standards, including the principles of equality and non-discrimination on the basis of sex, the right to life when the procedure results in death, and the right to freedom from torture or cruel, inhuman or degrading treatment or punishment. As it interferes with healthy genital tissue in the absence of medical necessity and can lead to severe consequences for a woman's physical and mental health, female genital mutilation is a violation of a person's right to the highest attainable standard of health(9). It also violates the rights of the child because many of them cannot enjoy child hood any more after this. Moreover, it distorts the sense of identity, brings in psychological consequences and their integrity.

Understanding FGM as a social convention provides insights as to why women, even though they have to suffer the consequences of being cut, favour its continuation. Most of them resist initiatives to end this because the abandonment is alleged to entail loss of status and protection. It is the ideology that succeeds in co-opting these women by the process of what Louis Althusser in his essay, "Ideology and Ideological State Apparatuses" has called as 'Interpellation' or 'hailing'. Althusser uses the term to explain the ways in which we get influenced by ideas and have effect on our lives; so much so that cultural ideas have such a hold on us that we believe they are our own. Interpellation is thus a process in which we encounter our culture's values and internalise them. These ideologies thus hail people and offer them a particular identity which is accepted as natural or obvious (699). Judith Butler's concept of how "[patriarchal] power imposes itself on us, and weakened by its force, we come to internalise or accept its terms" (2) which she theorised in *The Psychic Power of Life: Theories in Subjection* account to how these women themselves take an active part in their subjection only to maintain their identity or to stay alive.

Feminism and trauma studies have been linked and extended in such a way that fictional representations such as novels, poetry and stories become a platform for the women to express their own anxieties and trauma, thereby giving a reflection of their 'raw' self and to give voice to the victims of human rights violations of their own communities. The unusual language with a blend of culture, gender and other dominant factors helps to project the inner world of woman. As a result, there is always a room for memories, introspection, retrospection and dreadful remembrances that are shaded by pain, wound and sorrow. Literature represents the mental trauma of individuals – the social, political cultural and historical dimensions of trauma thereby restricting the tendency to limit the trauma to the realm of psychoanalytic studies.

Alice Walker is an Afro American woman writer who had explored the trauma of mutilation inflicted on the body as well in the mind of a woman in her novel *Possessing the Secret of Joy*. Walker wrote the entire fiction based on the life experiences of women characters maimed and unmade by female genital mutilation to create an awareness about the hazardous effects of the practice on women. The first-hand experience of having undergone the pain of mutilation and witnessing the trauma many women of her community have undergone have invoked in her the need to use literature as a resistant tool to 'right the wrong' and to reflect upon the suffering it induces upon the female body and psyche. Robbie J. Walker, in the article "Coping Strategies of the Women in Alice Walker's Novel: Implications of Survival", refers to Alice Walker's indictment regarding the plight of many women who are subjected to the cruel subjugation of many practices under the guise of culture and patriarchy. The article quotes Alice's own words thus: "women who are cruelty exploited, spirits and bodies mutilated, relegated to the most harrow and confining lives, [are] sometimes driven to madness" (405).She calls this practice as man's eternal desire to have control over woman and through this practice he controls both the body and mind of woman.

In the novel *Possessing the Secret of Joy,* Walker presents the story of Tashi who is African by birth and later moves to the United States where she finds herself stuck between the two cultures. This novel exemplifies the powerful impact of cultural interpellation upon the female subjects and how it traumatises them when they do not subject themselves to certain norms set for them. Female Genital Mutilation which has become a cultural reminder in Tashi's life and in her own society prompts her to undergo that odious act after she had reached the age of puberty. Even though she had fled from it initially, Tashi finds herself impure, abnormal and distinct from the other Olinkan woman as she had not undergone the 'rites of passage' which was an essential factor for being one with one's culture. This inner conflict between her own self and the cultural instincts to which she is bound to, puts herself in an identity crisis and as a part of finding herself to be a 'Complete Olinkan' she finally decided to go through the procedure with the help of a 'tsunga' woman named M'Lissa, who serves to be a traditional circumciser in the Olinkan village for centuries. It is only after the circumcision when she reaches U.S with her husband Adam and her sister-in-law Olivia, that she begins to realise the scorching effects and hazardous consequences of the circumcision which had altered her whole life thereafter.

Literature's power to expose the trauma inflicted upon its characters is clearly evident in a novel like *Possessing the Secret of Joy*. The writer completely accentuates the practice and horrors of female genital mutilation, a barbaric ritual practiced mostly on women and little children in African countries which have long lasting effects causing both physical and psychological trauma in their life. Trauma can be explained as an extrasensory wound or a distasteful experience which happens in the life of an individual thereby creating a physical or even an anomalous psychological stress. A much deeper analysis of trauma studies reveals that it is more concerned with the mental state of mind creating a deep impact in the overall life of a person after he or she had gone through a horrid experience. Trauma is the rupture of a border that places the inside and the outside into a strange reciprocity. It is, in other words a life endangering event that dislocates the preconceived notions about the world. Judith Herman in her work *Trauma and Recovery: The Aftermath of Violence* holds the opinion that "traumatic events generally involve threats of life or bodily integrity or close personal encounter with violence and death" (23). Transcending the boundaries of psychoanalysis, trauma studies as a new phenomenon makes a distinct role for itself in literature and the contemporary trauma theory testifies that it creates a divide or destruction in identity. A novel or any sort of literary work which explores the world of trauma through fictional characters or real ones make obvious how a traumatic event disrupts connection between self and others by avenging fundamental assumptions about societal relationships and laws which are morally connected. Culture which still continues to have dominant place in human life and the society as a whole influence us to an extent which may alter to cause a change in one's individual self. Trauma as a sudden or appalling event can occur at any point in life but when it is violence over the body which takes place in the early life of a woman, it turns out to produce scars which have deep physical and psychological consequences that last for a life time. Cathy Caruth in her *Unclaimed Experience: Trauma, Narrative and History* argues that "Trauma seems to be much more than a pathology or the simple illness of a wounded Psyche: It is always the story of a wound that cries out, that addresses us in the attempt to tell us of a reality or truth" (45). Such is the story of Tashi which Walker has weaved to represent all those young girls who have been irrevocably wounded by traditions that cause them much pain and deny them the freedom to fly, to flourish and may be drive them to madness.

Alice Walker has written the novel in a series of monologues where all the characters of the story express their own state of mind and reactions to the perilous event that had occurred in Tashi's life. The novel starts with Tashi saying "I did not realise for a long time that I was dead" (3), thereby giving the readers a hint of the sickened mental state of the protagonist. Later this takes the readers to the event that has wounded her psyche and leads her to such a conclusion. Tashi, an Olinkan by birth, had migrated to America after her marriage with Adam where she is renamed as Tashi Evelyn Johnson. The novel unfurls with the scene of Tashi awaiting in prison her capital punishment for murdering M'Lissa, a 'traditional tsunga' Olinkan woman who carries out the horrid practice of FGM. The crux of the story lies in the question of how and why M'Lissa has been murdered by Tashi, what has driven her to insanity, how memory is traumatic and how Tashi resists to the psychic 'split' that has occurred due to the traumatic event. This is unravelled by the subsequent monologues of her husband Adam, his sister Olivia, Lisette, Benny, Pierre and a few other characters. From the time when Tashi is a child in Africa to the late 1980's when Tashi is in the final stages of her life, the novel unknots the African patriarchal cultures that typically consider the female sexuality as something which is inferior, unclean and that which has to be preserved from being questioned by others.

Despite the social forces which pave way for such traumatic events that disrupts one's life causing a physical and emotional smash in them, trauma also has an inherently political, historical, cultural and ethical dimension. Simon de Beauvoir in her work *The Second Sex* argued that "One is not born, but rather becomes a woman" (21). As Judith Butler puts it in her work *Performativity, Precarity and Sexual Politics* "there is no gender without this reproduction of norms" (1). It is culture and society as a whole which has been instrumental in bringing this false consciousness into female psyche. It is this social construct and the forced commonality that made Tashi sacrifice herself for the tradition.

Tashi suffers from mental illness and uses story telling as a means to articulate the 'unspeakable'. She says "I told Raye about my lifelong tendency to escape from reality into the realm of fantasy and storytelling. Without this it would be impossible for me to guess anything out of the ordinary had happened to me" (Walker 124). Olivia, Tashi's lifelong friend and Adam's sister who is also an American missionary says that "This is the way Tashi expressed herself" (5) and takes over the narration by describing the day when herself and her brother Adam first met Tashi. The story is non-linear and moves to and fro in such a way as it connects Tashi's past and present through the monologues of different characters who are all closely connected in a way or the other. Tashi being in a psychiatric treatment at present tries to recall her past memories under the guidance of her 'white witch doctor.' At first, she recalls the story of her sister Dura, who once put a burning twig into her mouth and how she cried for help. Walkeralso explains Tashi witnessing the mutilation and the subsequent death of her sister Dura. Tashi narrates the events in such a way that it is seen as fragments piling up the past and present in between so that it confuses the reader at times and makes one realise the hazardous effects of the catastrophic event of FGM. This fragmented narrative is reflective of the fragmented self of Tashi, someone who had been shattered by the 'unkindest cut' and also a significant characteristic of trauma fiction. The question of what it takes for a subject to overcome PSTD requires special attention in trauma theory after which the violent trauma that the subject had gone through is questioned or phrased with the help of language. Compensating the lack of memory is sometimes difficult while narrating a traumatic event. One way to overcome this lack of form or memory is to use the similar fragmented narrative structures in narration so that it creates a mirror to the ruptured psyche-one that is disintegrated from the self, society and the external world.

The first ever shock that remained buried in Tashi's childhood memories was the death of her sister at the hands of the barbaric ritual FGM. However, surprisingly though aware of the live taking consequences, she had been perfectly interpellated by will to connect to her roots inspite of any European enlightenment. The fissure in Tashi's psyche was mainly due to the disparity between her expectation to be a complete Olinkian and the actual harmful effects of FGM on woman. She like many of the girls conditioned by cultural ties and who subject themselves to harmful cultural practices with little knowledge about it often turn paranoiac. After the act what loitered more in memory was the explicit details of the circumcision and its consequences rather than Tashi's emotions which is equally revealed through the monologues of other characters as well.

> It now took a quarter of an hour for her to pee. Her menstrual periods lasted ten days. She was incapacitated by cramps nearly half the month. There were premenstrual cramps: cramps caused by the near impossibility of flow passing through so tiny an aperture as M'Lissa had left, after fastening together the raw sides of Tashi's vagina with a couple of thorns and inserting a straw so that in healing, the traumatised flesh might not grow together, shutting the opening completely; cramps caused by residual flow that could not find its way out, was not reabsorbed into her body, and had nowhere to go. There was the odour too, of soured blood, which no about of scrubbing, until we got to America, ever washed off(Walker 61).

Olivia, her American missionary friend and Adam's sister was against Tashi's decision of cutting herself and counteracting her Tashi says: "Who are you and your people never to accept us as we are? Never to imitate any of our ways? It is always we who have to change" (Walker 21). Her only wish was to be a complete Olinkian not knowing what the barbaric act would induce upon her body and psyche.

Being an uncircumcised woman, it was her emotions that had driven her rather than her own intellect. Even though there were noticeable changes in the Olinkan society after the arrival of the missionaries which included the mumbled prayers and conversions of people Tashi found herself detached from both her American culture and her own African roots. As she says:

> Certainly, to all my friends who'd been circumcised, my uncircumcised vagina was thought of as a monstrosity. They laughed at me. Jeered at me for having a tail. I think they meant my labia majora. After all, none of them had vaginal lips; none of them had a clitoris; they had no idea what these things looked like; to them I was bound to look odd. There were a few other girls who had not been circumcised. The girls who had been would sometimes run from actually run from us, as if we were demons. Laughing, though. Always laughing. Besides, Our Leader, our Jesus Christ, said we must keep all our ways and that no Olinka man – in this he echoed the great liberator Kenyatta-would even think of marrying a woman who was not circumcised (Walker 113-14).

To remain uncircumcised in such a society leads her to a state of inconsistency which she considered as a taboo. Even talking about circumcision was a taboo in Olinkian culture. Though not forced to undergo the process during her teen ages as a result of the constant exhortation by the Christian missionaries, it was her deep inner wish to stay connected to her culture that made her to surrender to such a defiant act. But this so-called act never made her brave, instead invoked in her a living nightmare and a crack in her subsequent life. Married later to her childhood friend Adam, she finds that she cannot enjoy sexual intercourse, and childbearing becomes an unbearably painful ordeal. This traumatic history leads to bouts of depression and insanity, and it necessitates the intervention of psychotherapy. Adam later describes Tashi as "someone whose whole life was destroyed by the enactment of a ritual upon her which she had not been equipped to understand" (Walker 152). She describes the pain, fear and shock such a mutilation left into her psyche. When Adam meets her in the Mbele camp he looks at her as if he doesn't know whether to laugh or cry. She doesn't show any eagerness in welcoming him and feels thus: "My eyes see him but they do not register his being. Nothing runs out of my eyes to greet him. It is as if myself is hiding behind an iron door" (Walker 44).

"The scars on her face were nearly healed, but she still had to fan the flies away as they were attracted by the odour of her blood, eager to eat at the feast provided by her wounds," says Olivia about Tashi after their return to America. This marks her as someone who is "no longer cheerful or impish" and "that her soul had been dealt a mortal blow was plain to anyone who dared look into her eyes" (Walker 181). Even though everyone took notice of the scars on her face no one spoke of the hidden scar between Tashi's thin legs. Those gave her "the classic Olinka woman's walk, in which the feet appear to slide forward and are rarely raised above the ground" (182). It is after her arrival in the U.S that she was able to critically evaluate her own culture when she itself became a victim of it. The thought that mothers and foremothers of the Olinkian tribe, who are considered as the preservers of culture, were following nothing but a barbaric ritual, was a wisdom that came to Tashi only at the moment when she had to painfully deliver her baby out through the vagina which was tightly sewed after infabiluation. She could not bear the thought of the quick-stepping American nurses looking at her as if she were some creature beyond their imagination. Even the obstetrician did it in such a way that he found it difficult to make an opening large enough for the baby's head to come out. Tashi felt like "some small but vital part of his brain is crushed by their ordeal" (230).

Sometimes the traumatic event overwhelms the psyche and continues to haunt the victim. As a result, the repressed haunting memory becomes a repetition of the past or the subject feels a compulsion within him or her to repeat the incidents that are associated with that particular incident. Jonathan I. Bisson in his article "Post traumatic stress disorder" argues that an individual exposed to a traumatic event involving actual or threatened death or serious injury, or a threat to the physical integrity of self or others experiences certain PSTD symptoms like recurrent distressing dreams, Detachment or estrangement feelings, intrusive distressing recollections and so on(1). Tashi's mental state gets shifted after the terrific process through which she had gone through and she is distracted by the memory of her sister Dura's death. It is during her psychiatric treatment with the old man that the bitter reminiscences of that incident is brought in detail. She says, "I do not dare tell him about the dream I have every night that terrifies me" (Walker 24). Tashi gets psychologically affected by the disturbing dreams that she had seen each day and made her shiver out of fear. This unconsciousness and sudden irresistible fear is unveiled in the form of a painting as she was unable to recall the events through words. She started painting the picture of a giant cock and she realises that there is something its foot is holding between its toes. It reminded her of that day when the howls of pain and terror arouse from an isolated hut. She says:

> Underneath a tree, on the bare ground outside the hut, lay a dazed row of little girls, though to me they seemed not so little. They were all a few years older than me. Dura's age. Dura, however, was not among them; and I knew instinctively that it was Dura being held down and tortured inside the hut. Dura who made those inhuman shrieks that rent the air and chilled my heart. Abruptly, inside, there was silence. And then I saw M'Lissa shuffle out, dragging her lame leg, and at first I didn't realise she was carrying anything, for it was so insignificant and unclean that she carried it not in her fingers but between her toes. A chicken-a hen, not a cock – was scratching futilely in the dirt between the hut and the tree where other girls, their own ordeal over, lay. M'Lissa lifted her foot and flung this small object in the direction of the hen, and she, as if waiting for this moment, rushed toward M'Lissa's upturned foot, located the flung object in the air and then on the ground, and in one quick movement of beak and neck, gobbled it down(Walker 70-71).

Walker through the characters of Lisette, Tashi's co-wife, Pierre, Lisette's son and Raye, Tashi's psychologist brings home the fact that women are ill-treated and made to suffer all over the world in different ways where the ultimate result is a kind of physical and psychological trauma. While Pierre talks about how his mother Lisette met his father in Africa, he is reminded of the story of an old man named Torabe who married many girls. He did not love anyone in particular and finally when he married a young girl, she complained to her parents the next day: "...he had cut her open with a hunting knife on their wedding night, and gave her no opportunity to heal" (181) and "her father instructed her mother to convince her of her duty because she was Torabe's wife, her place was with him, her mother told her" (181). Walker through this story makes it clear that this is the general condition of women which still continues even today in certain parts of Africa. Pierre makes her realise the fact that 'it is the connection between mutilation and enslavement that is at the root of the domination of women in the world (185). Walker through this tale also informs that it is the supremacy of men over women that is reflected through the worst procedure of mutilation.

Tashi becomes physically challenged due to the inept way M'Lissa sewed her up after the procedure. It is during her psychiatric treatment that she learns from an article in *Newsweek* that M'Lissa was still alive and has become a national monument. The Olinkan government has honoured her for her restless service during the liberation wars. Tashi reaches a breaking point upon seeing the person whom she feels is responsible for the murder of her sister and for disrupting her own life and she returns to Africa to avenge for what M'Lissa had done to her. Tashi keeps fingering the razors kept secretly concealed under her pillow and fantasizes M'Lissa's bloody demise.

> I swore I would mutilate her wrinkled body so much her own God wouldn't recognise her. I smiled to think of her nose lying bloody on the bed. But each morning, like the storyteller Scheherazade M'Lissa told me another version of reality of which I had not heard (Walker 196).

M'Lissa who had circumcised many girls and inflicted pain upon them also reveals the reality of her own life when she was a victim of the barbaric practice. She tells Tashi, "I could never again see myself, for the child that finally rose from the mat three months later, and dragged herself out of initiation hut and finally home, was not the child who had been taken there. I was never to see that child again" (206).

She had never cried after that and the pain has reached a crescendo, as when a loud metal drum is struck with a corresponding metal stick, and "there is no god known to man who cares about children or about women. And that the God of woman is autonomy" (227). Even M'Lissa feels bitter of her tradition and that she calls

Tashi a 'fool'. Being a *tsunga,* she scorns at women who inflict pain on their bodies just for the sake of their men. She reveals the truth and puts it thus "Even the sweetest mango in my mouth is bitter to me... women are too cowardly to look behind a smiling face. A man smiles and tells them they will look beautiful weeping, and they send for the knife" (228).

Through the voice of M'Lissa, Walker openly criticises the patriarchal ties where women become blind victims who are forced to follow the tribal traditional values. She also unveils the fact that even today there are women who have paid the *tsungas* to make them tighter than as. African women are surrenders in a patriarchal and polygamous tribal society which has made female genital mutilation "sacred" and the village elders believe that God "created the tsunga" and so breaking this norm is a religious taboo. Even though the sad stories of M'Lissa kept Tashi's attempt of killing her at bay, she finally killed her by placing a pillow over her face rather than slashing her with the razors. She puts it thus:

> She told me it was traditional for a well-appreciated *tsunga* to be murdered by someone she circumcised, then burned. I carried out what was expected of me.... the traditional tribal society dealt so cleverly with its appreciation of the *tsunga* and its hatred of her. But of course the *tsunga* was to the traditional elders merely a witch they could control, an extension of their own dominating power (Walker 260).

She is convinced that "the little girls who are dying and the women too, are infected by the unwashed, unsterilised sharp stones, tin tops, bits of glass, rusty razors and grungy knives used by the tsunga" (204). By revealing the fact that almost every act of intercourse involves tearing and bleeding, Walker through the voice of Tashi points out that a woman after her circumcision undergoes a continuum of pain. Even when Adam pleads to the attorney to understand her wife who is physically and psychologically hurt, but not insane, the Jury rejects him saying "Mother Lissa was a monument! Your wife has murdered a monument. The Grandmother of the race!" (253).

Tashi towards the end of the novel is portrayed as a woman who tries hard for the betterment of her people. She scornfully says that the allotted role of the African is to suffer, to die and not to know why. The blind ignorance and acceptance of the Africans fate and forced patriarchal norms makes her to see herself in them. It is her own action, her own resistance to the rituals that mutilate the body and soul in the name of tradition and culture, that lead to her healing. And thus, at the end of the novel, Walker proudly reveals that "Resistance is the Secret of their joy" (Walker 264). It is for breaking the stillness encircling the misery of women's life in general and female circumcision in particular that Tashi had been punished rather than for killing M'Lissa. Alice Walker through the narrative voice of Tashi proclaims the suppression inflicted upon the blacks and also the brutal customs that define their race and culture while the progressive American woman, Evelyn, serves as the resistant voice speaking out against such vicious patriarchal ties.

Works Cited

"Eliminating Female Genital Mutation." World Health Organisation. www.un.org/womenwatch/daw/csw/csw52/statements_missions/Interagency_Statement_on_Eliminating_FGM.pdf

"Female Genital Mutation". World Health Organisation, www.who.int/news-room/fact-sheets/detail/female-genital-mutilation.

Althusser, Louis. *Ideology and Ideological state Apparatus*, 1970.

Bisson, Jonathan I. "Post-traumatic Stress Disorder". *Occupational Medicine,* vol. 57, No. 6,2007, pp.399-403, doi.org/10.1093/occmed/kqm069

Bordo, Susan. *Unbearable Weight: Feminism, Western Culture and the Body.* U of California P, 2004.

Butler, Judith. *Performativity, Precarity and Sexual Politics.* U of California P, 2015.

De Beauvoir, Simone. *The Second Sex.*Vintage, 1949

Caruth, Cathy. *Unclaimed Experience: Trauma, Narrative and History.* The John Hopkins UP, 1996.

Herman, Judith. *Trauma and Recovery: The Aftermath of Violence.* Basic Books, 1992.

Walker, Robbie J. "Coping Strategies of the women in Alice Walker's Novel: Implications of Survival", *CLA Journal,* vol. 30. no. 4, pp. 401-418.

Walker, Alice. *Possessing the Secret of Joy.* Vintage, 1992.

Contributors

1. **Priya K. Nair** is Assistant Professor of English at St. Teresa's College Ernakulam, Kerala. She has translated T. D. Ramakrishnan's award winning Malayalam novel into English, *Sugandhi Alias Andal Devanayaki.* She has also translated Dr B. Umadathan's autobiography into English, *Dead Men Tell Tales: The Memoir of a Police Surgeon* Her research interests include Culture Studies, Literary Theory and Translation Studies.
2. **Arunlal K.** is an author, translator and speaker who currently work as Assistant Professor at the Department of English, Government College Mokeri, Kerala. His doctoral work is in Cultural Studies from the English and Foreign Languages University Hyderabad, and has worked with the faculty of Humanities at NIT Warangal until 2010. He has worked for the International Shakespearean Desk's project, on Localising Shakespeare. He has written and published widely on issues concerning culture, philosophy and literature.
3. **Rajesh V. Nair** is Assistant Professor of English at School of Letters, Mahatma Gandhi University, Kerala. He has published essays on areas such as life writing, graphic narratives, memory studies, popular culture and gender. His current projects include an introductory book on Life Writing and essays on transgender autobiographies and street theatre.
4. **Joji John Panicker** is a bilingual writer, poet, critic, academician, editor. He works as Assistant Professor of English at CMS College (Autonomous) Kottayam, Kerala. His areas of interest are Indian Writing in English, Postcolonial studies and Cultural Studies. He is the Joint Secretary of the Guild of Indian English Writers Editors and Critics.
5. **Kochurani Joseph** is Assistant Professor of English at T. M. Jacob Memorial Government College, Manimalakunnu, Koothattukulam, Kerala. She is a research scholar at Mahatma

Gandhi University, Kottayam, Kerala. Her areas of interest are Migration and Refugee literature.

6. **Smitha M. is** Assistant Professor of English at Maharaja's College, Ernakulam. Her primary area of research is film studies, especially postcolonial Indian Cinema. She has both academic and creative writings published in various journals, books and magazines.
7. **Smrithi Venugopal** is a Senior Research Fellow in English pursuing research in the Post Graduate and Research Department of English, St. Joseph's College (Autonomous), Devagiri, Calicut.
8. **Navya Chandran** is Assistant Professor of English at Cochin College, Kerala. She is pursuing research at Mahatma Gandhi University, Kottayam, Kerala. She is interested in Digital Humanities, Visual Studies, Graphic Medicine and Trauma Studies.
9. **Indu V. Nandakumar** is Assistant Professor of English at Government Polytechnic College, Cherthala, Kerala. She is a research scholar at Mahatma Gandhi University, Kottayam, Kerala. Gender studies and trauma studies are her areas of academic enquiry.
10. **Geethu V. Nandakumar** is a poet and researcher interested in Women's Studies, Gender Studies and Trauma Studies. She holds a Post Graduate Degree in English Language and Literature from CMS College, Kottayam, Kerala.

Index